"*The Upward Spiral* approach to well-being blends the best of cutting
by-step instructions for improving your life. Alex Korb is a scientis
encouraging teacher, who in this workbook offers you grounded wa
ease anxiety and melt away depression to live a more meaningful, connected, and inspiring life
ahead."

> —**Daniel J. Siegel, MD**, *New York Times* bestselling author of *Aware*

"*The Upward Spiral* is a helpful and eminently sensible approach to changing the thoughts and behaviors associated with depression. Alex Korb provides a practical guide for getting a handle on the disruption and pain caused by this common and painful condition."

> —**Kay Redfield Jamison**, author of *An Unquiet Mind*, and Pulitzer Prize finalist for
> *Robert Lowell, Setting the River on Fire*

"Deeply practical and effective tools based in science to not only grow strengths for resiliency around anxiety and depression—but also boost your skills for happiness."

> —**Elisha Goldstein, PhD**, author of *Uncovering Happiness*

"This easy-to-read book is chock-full of simple-to-do, scientifically supported ideas and exercises to overcome depression. Can you benefit from Korb's techniques to train your brain to adopt new thinking and acting patterns that can also prevent depression from coming back? Let's see. Change your facial expression as if you were smiling. If you can do this, you can do the antidepression exercises in this book. As you test new, helpful ideas and habit-forming actions, you may soon enough find the powerlessness thinking of pessimism replaced by the powerful thinking of realistic optimism. At that point, here is a question for you: What did I learn by taking charge of my own progress?"

> —**William Knaus, EdD**, author of *The Cognitive Behavioral Workbook for Depression* and
> *The Cognitive Behavioral Workbook for Anxiety*

"*The Upward Spiral Workbook* is grounded in the same excellent neuroscience principles as *The Upward Spiral* but offers even more practical guidance to enacting meaningful life changes for alleviating depression and maintaining recovery. While I recognize its value in self-help, as a physician I'm also excited to use this workbook as part of a comprehensive treatment plan for my patients."

> —**Helen Mayberg, MD**, director of the Center of Advanced Circuit Therapeutics, and
> professor in the departments of neurology, neurosurgery, psychiatry, and neuroscience
> at the Icahn School of Medicine at Mount Sinai

"Alex Korb has empowered consumers to understand their neurophysiology and to take charge of their mental operating systems in order to develop new habits of body, mind, and spirit. Such changes reverse the downward spiral into depression. We face an epidemic of depression and suicide. Consumers want more than just pills and talk therapy. They need an array of evidence-based approaches they can use every day. Use this program, find what works for you, and change your life."

—**Richard P. Brown, MD**, coauthor of *The Healing Power of the Breath* and *Complementary and Integrative Treatments in Psychiatric Practice*

"I fully love this workbook, it helps you to understand what is happening in our (sometimes) crazy brains in a really easy and fun way. Alex Korb inspired me to build my mindfulness app, Happy Not Perfect, after he was the first one to teach me how to cope with my emotions. Science meets emotional health, a recipe everyone needs to know about! This book can help you manage many different aspects of your life."

—**Poppy Jamie**, founder of Happy Not Perfect

"Most books about happiness are so loaded with trite platitudes that they make me miserable. *The Upward Spiral Workbook* is a delightful exception. Alex Korb delivers actionable insights from the latest neuroscience in the most warm and accessible of ways. This practical yet intimate guide provides concrete steps toward a more positive outlook—and a better life."

—**Eric Barker**, *Wall Street Journal* best-selling author of *Barking Up the Wrong Tree*

"Alex Korb is a genius. It's easy to find an extremely clever neuroscientist, but what is rare, is finding a neuroscientist who can translate their knowledge into actionable advice and compelling metaphors. This book is packed with things I didn't know, from fascinating facts about the architecture of sleep, to why exercise is like marijuana for the brain, to why sunglasses reduce tension. Brilliant."

—**Catherine Gray**, author of *The Unexpected Joy of Being Sober* and *The Unexpected Joy of Being Single*

"Filled with tangible practices and rooted in research, *The Upward Spiral Workbook* is an accessible resource for anyone dealing with the stress and anxiety of modern life. I welcome its focus on helping the reader to understand not only why they may feel what they feel, but also *how* they may begin to shift—and doing this with self-compassion and without self-recrimination."

—**Nataly Kogan**, author of *Happier Now*

"Alex Korb makes the reader feel he is talking directly to *them*, as he compassionately combats the common beliefs people hold about depression and anxiety that serve as barriers to getting better—such as, *It's my fault*; *I should be able to snap out of it*; *I am the only person feeling this way*; *I should be over my childhood traumas already*. Although Korb provides wonderful and insightful exercises for getting better, his approach is unique and wise in continually emphasizing the importance of the 'inner work' people need to do to alter their false and self-defeating beliefs."

—**Regina Pally, MD**, psychiatrist, author of *The Reflective Parent*, and founder and codirector of the Center for Reflective Communities

"Alex Korb is a master at translating the complexities of the brain. The step-by-step actions in each chapter are extremely helpful for anyone who wrestles with anxiety or depression. What impressed me most about this book is he provides simple strategies that anyone can do. As you work through his easy-to-do exercises, you will actively transform your brain and you *will* feel better. This wonderful workbook is the perfect addition to *The Upward Spiral*."

—**Jonas Horwitz, PhD**, licensed psychologist, and author of *How to Stop Feeling So Damn Depressed*

"This companion workbook to *The Upward Spiral* offers excellent, evidence-based, practical tools in an easy to use and understand format. It should be immensely helpful for anyone suffering from depression or other challenging emotions."

—**Diana Winston**, director of mindfulness education at the UCLA Mindful Awareness Research Center, and coauthor of *Fully Present*

The Upward Spiral

WORKBOOK

ALEX KORB, PhD

New Harbinger Publications, Inc.

Publisher's Note

This publication is designed to provide accurate and authoritative information in regard to the subject matter covered. It is sold with the understanding that the publisher is not engaged in rendering psychological, financial, legal, or other professional services. If expert assistance or counseling is needed, the services of a competent professional should be sought.

NEW HARBINGER PUBLICATIONS is a registered trademark of New Harbinger Publications, Inc.

Distributed in Canada by Raincoast Books

Copyright © 2019 by Alex Korb
New Harbinger Publications, Inc.
5674 Shattuck Avenue
Oakland, CA 94609
www.newharbinger.com

Cover design by Amy Shoup

Acquired by Elizabeth Hollis Hansen

Edited by Brady Kahn

Illustrations on pages 10, 12, 13, and 14 by Alexis Frederick-Frost

All Rights Reserved

Library of Congress Cataloging-in-Publication Data on file

Printed in the United States of America.

23   22   21

10   9   8   7   6   5   4

In memory of Dr. Billi Gordon—remain fabulous and phenomenal.

Contents

Foreword

Depression is a terrible condition that impacts far too many people every year, creating a profound impact on both individuals and their communities. As a psychiatrist, I understand the importance of utilizing the latest medical interventions in the treatment of mental health conditions, but I'm also frustrated by their limitations. I have studied neuroscience and depression for over forty years and have come to understand that medicine alone cannot adequately address the complexity of human depression.

In his excellent first book, *The Upward Spiral,* Dr. Korb illuminated the brain processes that lead to depression and provided a few helpful suggestions to getting better. This workbook extends and complements *The Upward Spiral,* focusing less on what's happening in the brain and more on what you can do about it. It is more prescriptive, offering actionable suggestions and exercises that you can implement in your daily life.

At the Semel Institute for Neuroscience and Human Behavior at UCLA, we are developing cutting-edge treatments for depression, anxiety, and other related disorders. However, from my many decades as a researcher and clinician, I've learned that some of the most powerful treatments for depression exist in a person's own thoughts and actions. With all the world-class neuroscience research that I oversee, it has become apparent that the chemistry and activity of the human brain is inextricably linked with human behavior. That is why I welcome this wonderful workbook.

In this practical and powerful guide, Dr. Korb leads the reader through explanations and exercises designed to provide a better understanding of the brain and how to use that understanding to reverse the course of depression. This book is about making small changes in your actions and thinking patterns that positively impact your brain activity and chemistry. It is full of useful exercises, interventions, and tips that are all backed by scientific research. Some of these interventions are recent, and others have been around for decades, even centuries, with neuroscience just starting to catch up in explaining why they work.

As both a scientist and a clinician, I recognize the importance of using evidence-based treatments as well as the difficulty of translating interventions from the lab to the real world. Dr. Korb has done an elegant job of combining the theory of neuroscience with the useful tools that provide a path to getting better.

I am pleased to welcome you to this book. *The Upward Spiral Workbook* offers a novel pathway in combating depression.

—Peter C. Whybrow, MD
Director, Semel Institute, UCLA
Author of *A Mood Apart* and *The Well-Tuned Brain*

Introduction

There are many ways you may have come to this book. Maybe it was recommended by a friend, or maybe you just stumbled across it in the bookstore (I hope those still exist by the time you're reading this). Maybe you read my previous book *The Upward Spiral* and enjoyed it, and you want more specific guidance about what to do.

Maybe things feel out of sorts, and you can't quite put your finger on what's wrong. Maybe this feeling came out of nowhere or was precipitated by some calamity. Maybe everything is too painful, and nothing seems worth the effort it requires. Maybe you're feeling an emptiness where your emotions should be—helpless, guilty, lost, and alone. Maybe you are overwhelmed by an ever-present sense of dread, or when you close your eyes at night, sleep just lingers on the perimeter, taunting you.

Whatever made you pick this book up, it suggests that there's some curiosity in you—a drive toward understanding and improvement. And that's the most important element to overcoming depression, anxiety, or whatever is holding you down.

The brain is malleable and can be reshaped, and thus so can the neural circuits that contribute to depression and anxiety. Even learning that basic fact reduces stigma and decreases pessimism (Lebowitz & Ahn, 2012, 2015). So you could stop right here, and you'd be better off than when you started, but there's still so much more that can help you.

Research has shown that depression is a problem with communication amongst the thinking, feeling, and action circuits in the brain. It is the product of certain interactions between the neural circuits of stress, habits, decision-making, and more.

Depression and anxiety are *downward spirals*: patterns of negative, unhealthy activity and reactivity that the brain ends up stuck in. There isn't one big solution to these downward spirals, but, using the exercises in this book, you can start to turn things around.

Recent research has uncovered the power of the *upward spiral*: the fact that small positive life changes lead to positive brain changes in its electrical activity, its chemical composition, and even its ability to grow new neurons. And these positive brain changes make further positive life changes more accessible. Upward spirals can reverse the downward patterns of depression and anxiety: helping to boost your mood and energy levels, improving the quality of your sleep, enhancing your sense of calm and connection, and reducing stress, anxiety, and even physical pain.

Whether you're suffering from depression or anxiety, addiction, insomnia, or chronic pain, there's hope. Because these conditions all rely on the same underlying brain circuits and chemicals, the same neuroscience applies. So if you want to understand what you can do to alter the neural circuits that control your mood and stress and habits and energy and sleep, then you've come to the right place.

I'll give you the big secret right up front. It might sound totally obvious or deeply profound, but regardless, it has the power to change your brain and your life. Simply put, by making small changes in your thoughts, actions, interactions, and environment, it's possible to change the activity and chemistry of the key brain circuits underlying depression and anxiety.

This workbook will help you gain a better understanding of your brain so that you can improve your mood, reduce your anxiety, and live the life you want to live. You'll learn about the basics of your brain, and how you can modify the neural circuits of depression and anxiety using simple life changes across a wide array of life domains, including physical activity, sleep, mindfulness, gratitude, and more. I will guide you through numerous exercises that have been scientifically proven to help boost mood and energy levels, improve the quality of sleep, reduce stress, and more. The research shows that you have the power to reshape your brain and reverse the course of depression.

The Parts of This Book

I admit that I don't know your life or the unique challenges you face, but I do know one thing for sure: you have a human brain (although if you're a highly intelligent giraffe or something else, I sincerely apologize); and this means we know why your brain sometimes gets stuck in depression or anxiety and, more importantly, what you can do about it.

This book starts with a brief introduction to the brain circuits that contribute to depression and anxiety. Chapter 1 introduces a lot of brain terms, but even if you can't remember the specifics, there's no need to fret. They'll get repeated over and over until they stick. And if you don't care about the specifics, that's fine too. The exercises in this book will still work.

The rest of the chapters guide you through a series of research-backed interventions that alter the activity and chemistry of key brain circuits, providing you with a toolkit for addressing the challenges you face. While each chapter is labeled with a specific spiral—"The Movement Spiral," "The Sleep Spiral," and so on—the distinction is somewhat artificial, because they are not fully separable.

The interventions, and the brain regions they target, are all interconnected, and the effects of each permeate into the others. For example, there's a chapter on gratitude, a chapter on sleep, and a chapter on social interactions. But, in fact, gratitude improves sleep quality, and it also helps you feel more connected with other people. Mindfulness can help change habits. Setting goals can make it easier to exercise, which can improve sleep quality, and so on.

All this is to say that the information in this book isn't neatly linear, because your brain isn't neatly linear. (There are also additional, supplementary materials available for download at the website for this book: http://www.newharbinger.com/42426. See the very back of this book for more details.) There is no single solution to depression, just like there is no single way to live a good life. Your brain is different from others, so your path will be different.

As you read through the book, don't try to implement every exercise in each chapter as you go. It would be overwhelming. Select the exercises that arouse your curiosity or challenge your thinking or feel manageable. You also don't have to read these chapters sequentially. It's perfectly fine to try an intervention from, say, chapter 7 before you try one from chapter 3, if you think it will be better for you at this point in time or even if it just feels more accessible. But do implement at least one exercise from each chapter before moving on, and as you spiral up, you can return to previous chapters to practice things you skipped. After reading chapter 1, you can start anywhere. I've laid out what I think the clearest path is, but part of this book is understanding the needs of your own brain.

Understanding is, in fact, one of two essential components; the other is *doing*. There is a key difference between understanding that physical activity is good for you and actually going for a brisk walk in the dwindling twilight and breathing in the deep and tranquil air.

This isn't a regular book—it's a workbook. I'm going to ask you to do things and write things down, and that's not just for fun. Enacting the suggestions in this book actually changes the brain in measurable ways. Actions, including writing, modify the brain in a different way than thoughts do, and both thoughts and actions are essential to fully capitalizing on the neuroscience of the upward spiral.

The good news is that you already have tools to help yourself—ways of dealing with stress, improving your mood, and managing your relationships. You might not be using those tools as effectively as you could, or the tools that you have may be incomplete—like a set of wrenches missing a few key sizes, essential but not always helpful in every situation. This book will provide you with additional tools, ones based on scientific evidence and developed by world-class psychologists, clinicians, researchers, and neuroscientists.

This book is an opportunity for self-reflection and personal growth. It is an opportunity for scientific experimentation on yourself. I'll provide you with the types of interventions that have been shown to help with depression and anxiety, and you can discover which ones are most helpful for you.

The exercises in this book are about simple life changes, from moving your body to keeping a gratitude journal. While some may seem sillier than others, all are backed by rigorous scientific research. They all support the goal of this book, which is to get you back on track, living the kind of life you want to live and being the kind of person you want to be. You don't always get to choose your challenges in life, but you do get to choose how you face them.

The Journey Begins

We're at the start of a journey. Sure, I'm here sitting in front of my laptop typing away from the safety of my office, and you're doing all the hard work, but I'll be there as a guide. And speaking of guides, don't think you need to do this all on your own. A therapist, doctor, or coach can help you implement the suggestions in this book or provide alternative treatments that you can't do on your own. There is no one right way—just many ways to create an upward spiral.

It's probably not going to be easy or straightforward. There will almost certainly be setbacks, but that's okay, because you're heading somewhere important.

And even to be where you are right now, you've already taken some important steps. While the future is unknown and uncertain, you created an intention (conscious or not) to get better, and by reading this book, you're proving to yourself that you mean it (chapter 7). You've got the right neural circuits and chemicals to get you back on track (chapter 1). So take a deep breath (chapter 4), and here we go.

Chapter 1

The Understanding and Awareness Spiral

Tennis legend Arthur Ashe once said, "To achieve greatness, start where you are, use what you have, do what you can." The same applies to overcoming depression. Start where you are. Use what you have. Do what you can. And to start where you are, you first have to understand where exactly that is. That includes taking stock of the thoughts and emotions swirling through your head, as well as understanding the neuroscience behind them. That's what this chapter is all about.

Think of this chapter as reading a guidebook before traveling in a new country. These preparations will help you understand what's happening in your brain and see how the interventions in the following chapters will help.

What Is Depression?

To put it simply, depression is a problem with how the thinking, feeling, and action circuits in the brain are communicating with and regulating each other. The brain gets stuck in particular patterns of activity and reactivity—thinking and acting in ways that keep you depressed. And once it's stuck, it's hard to get unstuck.

Unfortunately, some people's brains are more sensitive to getting stuck in a downward spiral of depression and anxiety. And it might not be whom you'd expect. It's common to think that the people most at risk for depression are those with lives full of hardship. Yes, negative life events, like losing a job or losing a spouse, can precipitate depression, but so can any big life change, like going to college, retiring, or moving to a new city. But importantly, depression is often more about the inherent workings of your brain than it is about external circumstances.

Are you a perfectionist? What is your response to stress? Are you aware of your feelings, or do you push them down deep? Do you find it difficult to receive help from others? Do your emotions overwhelm you, even positive emotions? Are you unrealistically optimistic? Or maybe you're pessimistic, and it affects your motivation. These characteristics are caused by subtle differences in brain circuits and can increase the risk for your brain getting stuck in a downward spiral of depression.

Depression is rooted in biology. It's not just something you can snap out of. If you could just snap out of it, then sort of by definition it wouldn't be depression. Let's try it. Just snap out of it!

Did that work? Great! You can stop reading this book. But otherwise, keep reading.

If depression isn't something you can snap out of, what do you do about it? Well, just because depression has biological underpinnings does not mean that it's set in stone. It's more like set in saltwater taffy—firm yet malleable.

Your neurobiology can be reshaped. Recognizing that depression is related to neurobiology can help reduce stigma and blame. And recognizing that your neurobiology is malleable has long-term benefits and gives you the possibility to help yourself (Lebowitz & Ahn, 2015).

Depression doesn't look the same for everyone, and neither does the path out of depression. This book will help you gain a better understanding of yourself, your neurobiology, and what works for you.

Do You Have Depression?

Filling out the nine-item Patient Health Questionnaire (PHQ-9) can help identify whether you might be suffering from clinical depression. Note that a mental health professional is needed for a diagnosis (and can also be very helpful in dealing with depression). But regardless of diagnosis, this book can be useful in dealing with symptoms. Importantly, if you are experiencing thoughts that life isn't worth living, then please talk to someone right away: a mental health professional, friend, or family member, or call 1-800-SUICIDE (784-2433).

Over the last 2 weeks, how often have you been bothered by any of the following problems?	Not at all	Some days	More than half the days	Nearly every day
1. Little interest or pleasure in doing things	0	1	2	3
2. Feeling down, depressed, or hopeless	0	1	2	3
3. Trouble falling asleep, staying asleep, or sleeping too much	0	1	2	3
4. Feeling tired or having little energy	0	1	2	3
5. Poor appetite or overeating	0	1	2	3
6. Feeling bad about yourself—or that you're a failure or have let yourself or your family down	0	1	2	3
7. Trouble concentrating on things, such as reading the newspaper or watching television	0	1	2	3
8. Moving or speaking so slowly that other people could have noticed. Or, the opposite—being so fidgety or restless that you have been moving around a lot more than usual	0	1	2	3
9. Thoughts that you would be better off dead or of hurting yourself in some way	0	1	2	3

Column totals:　_____ + _____ + _____ + _____

Grand total = _____

Evaluate the total. A sum of 5 to 9 represents mild depression, 10 to 14 represents moderate depression, 15 to 19 represents moderately severe depression, and 20 and higher represents severe depression.

Regardless of the severity, take a moment to think about how your problems make it difficult for you to do your work, take care of things at home, or get along with other people. This will help you to get a clearer idea of how much your depression is getting in the way of what's important to you.

There's a lot of overlap between depression and anxiety, with the majority of people with depression also having issues with anxiety, and vice versa (Lamers et al., 2011). As you start to learn more about the underlying neurobiology, why this is will start to become clearer. There's also a lot of overlap with related disorders like chronic pain, insomnia, and addiction.

Do You Have Anxiety?

This is the generalized anxiety disorder questionnaire (GAD-7). It was initially developed to help in the diagnosis of generalized anxiety disorder but can also help identify whether you might be suffering from many types of anxiety. While, again, a mental health professional is needed for a diagnosis, this book can be useful in dealing with anxiety symptoms.

Over the last 2 weeks, how often have you been bothered by any of the following problems?	**Not at all**	**Some days**	**More than half the days**	**Nearly every day**
1. Feeling nervous, anxious, or on edge	0	1	2	3
2. Not being able to stop or control worrying	0	1	2	3
3. Worrying too much about different things	0	1	2	3
4. Trouble relaxing	0	1	2	3
5. Being so restless that it is hard to sit still	0	1	2	3
6. Becoming easily annoyed or irritable	0	1	2	3
7. Feeling afraid as if something awful might happen	0	1	2	3

Column totals: _____ + _____ + _____ + _____

Grand total = _____

Evaluate the total. A sum of 5 to 9 represents mild anxiety, 10 to 14 represents moderate anxiety, and 15 or higher represents severe anxiety.

Even though you're reading a self-help book, it's important to remember that you don't have to do everything on your own. If you're experiencing difficulties with depression or anxiety, a mental health professional can provide even more help and guidance than fits in this book.

A Map of the Brain

Again, depression and anxiety are both primarily a result of communication amongst the emotion, thinking, and action circuits in the brain—how they are interacting with and regulating, or failing to regulate, each other. These circuits can be described respectively as the limbic system, prefrontal cortex, and striatum.

One easy way to begin to understand these brain regions is to know how they evolved. We'll start from the inside out, because in the brain, the deepest parts are the most ancient.

First, let's go all the way back to the dinosaurs. They had a brain stem, which sits at the base of the skull and controls the basic functions for staying alive, such as breathing and regulating blood pressure. Just above that is a circuit for controlling actions and movements called the *striatum*. They also had the beginnings of some basic emotional circuitry called the *limbic system*, but that's about it. So the Tyrannosaurus rex had a huge head, but not much rattling around in there.

Then around a hundred million years ago, the first mammals popped up with more brain-power. The emotional limbic system continued to evolve, allowing for a greater range of emotions and actions. But importantly, another layer of brain tissue began to expand around the reptilian brain, one that held amazing processing capabilities: the *cortex*.

The word "cortex" simply means surface, and as mammals continued to evolve, we got more and more of it. Rats and squirrels have very little cortex. Dogs and cats have a bit more, and monkeys even more still. Over millions of years, as the brain grew bigger and bigger, the cortex essentially had to get squished to fit inside the head, like crumpling up a newspaper, which is why the surface of the human brain looks so wrinkled.

The part of the cortex near the front of the head (the aptly named *frontal cortex*) became really good at processing complex situations. In particular, the part in the very front, called the *prefrontal cortex*, is a very powerful computer and deals with planning, abstract thought, decision making, and social interactions. The prefrontal cortex is the part of the brain that makes us most uniquely human, and percentage-wise, we've got more than any other animal.

You don't need to memorize all these brain regions. It's helpful just to get the big picture that there's a brain region responsible for your emotions and another brain region responsible for planning and thinking. If you find the scientific names overwhelming, distracting, or even uninteresting, then whenever you see a word like "limbic system" or "prefrontal cortex," just replace it in your mind with *brain region*.

The Habitual and Impulsive Striatum

Over two thousand years ago, the Greek philosopher Heraclitus wrote, "It is hard to fight against impulsive desire; whatever it wants it will buy at the cost of the soul." While the ancient Greeks didn't have a strong understanding of neuroscience, they were definitely on to something.

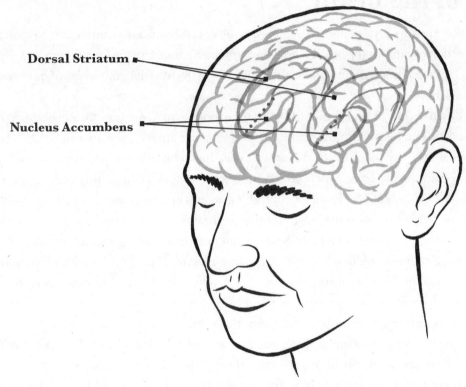

Dorsal Striatum

Nucleus Accumbens

Figure 1. Striatum

Deep inside the brain is a set of circuits devoted to actions and movement: the striatum, which is divided into an upper part and a lower part that do slightly different things (see figure 1). The *dorsal striatum*—the upper part—is involved in habits: the things you do automatically, without thinking, in a stimulus-response type way. Each time you repeat an action, it gets wired more strongly in the dorsal striatum, making it more likely that you'll do it again. The activity in the dorsal striatum is what makes you put on your seat belt when you get in the car or brush your teeth before bed. Unfortunately, it's also the reason that you might reach for a beer when you get stressed or feel rejected when a friend doesn't immediately respond to your messages. The dorsal striatum controls not only physical habits but also social and emotional habits.

By contrast, the *nucleus accumbens*—the lower part of the striatum—is involved in impulsive actions. The nucleus accumbens wants to do things that are new, exciting, and immediately pleasurable. The nucleus accumbens is the reason that you'd want to have sex and eat chocolate, maybe at the same time, for better or worse. Sometimes impulsive actions are fun and enjoyable, but sometimes they get in the way of your long-term goals.

The thing to keep in mind is that both parts of the striatum follow a different logic than the more evolved parts of the brain. They're not good or bad; they're just the way they are. They might make certain things easier or more difficult, but they're not trying to harm you. In fact, they're trying to help you. Living your life would be impossible without routines or impulses. Ultimately, the specific routines and impulses you've come to adopt may not always be the most adaptive, but you can change them over time.

It's helpful to think of the striatum as a dog. It does what it can to get a treat, and it needs to be trained. Maybe your dog is getting a bit old and has acquired a few bad habits, and it might be harder to teach new tricks. Over the course of your life, you've been training your dorsal striatum to act in a particular way, so it's hard to change. But it's still possible through *neuroplasticity*: the ability of the brain to be reshaped. You just need a reason. And treats. And time.

The Emotional Limbic System

Still deep in the brain, but not as evolutionarily ancient as the striatum, sits an important group of structures essential for joy and fear and memory and motivation (see figure 2). This is the limbic system, and it acts like a small child: if it doesn't get exactly what it wants when it wants, then it's liable to throw a tantrum.

At the heart of the limbic system is a structure called the *hypothalamus*, which is essential in maintaining homeostasis. If you can't remember your ninth grade biology class, *homeostasis* is the body's need to maintain a fairly constant internal environment. While your external environment can vary drastically from a dry frozen tundra to a sweaty nightclub, you need homeostasis to keep everything inside you relatively balanced. So when you need air, water, food, or anything else to stay alive, the hypothalamus kicks into action and triggers the stress response.

While "stress" sounds like a bad word, it's not. Stress is simply a response to changes in your environment. There's nothing inherently bad about stress. Stress is bad only if it overwhelms your ability to cope. A common solution is to reduce stress, but increasing your ability to cope is also helpful.

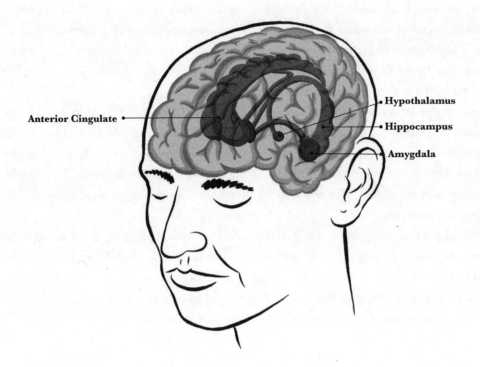

Figure 2. Limbic System

Closely connected to the hypothalamus is an almond-shaped structure called the amygdala. The *amygdala* is often called the fear center of the brain, but it's important in all strong emotions. It's one of the primary danger detectors in the brain, trying to figure out what might harm you, or what might make you need to use your stress response. It does not think rationally but instead relies on past experiences and probabilities to help give you a gut feeling about a situation.

Also closely connected with the hypothalamus—and immediately adjacent to the amygdala—sits the *hippocampus,* which is the main processor for memory. It's not where memories are stored, but it's important in recording them for the long term. It's also really important in understanding and recognizing the context that you're in. If you're walking through a big field of grass and get attacked by a lion, the hippocampus is going to commit that to long-term memory. So the next time you're walking through the same field, the hippocampus is going to perk up and say, "Hey, this seems familiar," and nudge the rest of the limbic system to be on high alert.

The hippocampus tries to generalize so that you can learn from previous situations. So maybe next time you're walking through any big field, the hippocampus might think that it seems familiar and use what it learned. But sometimes it overgeneralizes.

That's a good thing if you walk into the street as a kid and almost get hit by a car; you want the hippocampus to generalize to all streets. But too much generalizing can be unhelpful. For example, say you get stuck in the elevator in your friend's apartment building. It might actually be helpful to be a little skeptical of that elevator next time and take the stairs instead. But it's not helpful to develop a fear of all elevators or of all small spaces. With too much generalizing in the hippocampus, a traumatic event can get carried with you everywhere.

The last main piece of the limbic system is the *anterior cingulate cortex*, which plays a really important role in attention. It notices pain and mistakes and anything that's relevant to you and to what you're trying to accomplish. Sometimes it seems like it distracts you with alerts about pain and mistakes, but it's just trying to be helpful.

While strong emotions involve the limbic system, they also rely on other parts of the brain. A sinking feeling in your stomach, a racing heart—these physical sensations from the body are processed by a region that is closely connected to the limbic system but not technically a part of it. It's called the *insula*, and it's a deep part of the cortex that deals with information from your heart, stomach, and other internal organs (see figure 3). The insula provides the physical experience of your emotions.

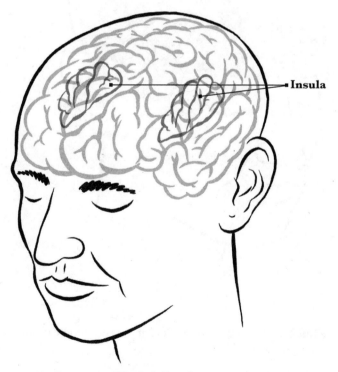

Figure 3. Insula

The emotional circuitry in your brain is essential to living the full breadth of the human emotional experience. But when it gets fatigued and starts draining the emotions from everything, or when it gets caught in a downward spiral, it's helpful to have some regulation. And that's where the more evolved parts of the brain come in handy.

The Thoughtful Prefrontal Cortex

The prefrontal cortex (PFC) is the most evolutionarily advanced part of the brain. The PFC is essentially the surface of the front third of the brain (see figure 4). It allows us to plan and make decisions and to be flexible—controlling our impulses or managing our emotions. It creates goals and intentions.

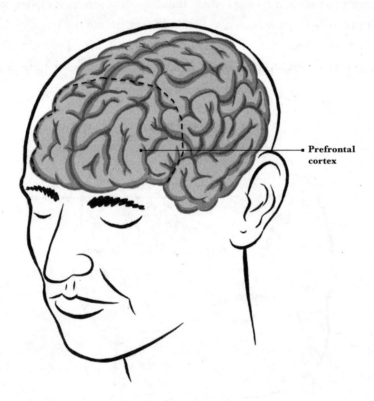

Prefrontal cortex

Figure 4. Prefrontal Cortex

Since it is such a huge part of the brain, different parts of it do different things. The upper part is more devoted to thoughts, while the lower part is more devoted to emotions. But whereas the limbic system is deeply involved in the feeling of emotions, the lower part of the PFC (*ventral*) is essential in thinking about emotions. This part of the PFC has lots of connections with the limbic system, while the upper (dorsal) part has lots of connections with the dorsal striatum and nucleus accumbens. So regardless of whether you're trying to tone down your emotions or get more excited, or control your impulses or habits or create new ones, the prefrontal cortex is involved.

If the striatum is a puppy running around, and the limbic system is a small child, then the PFC is the adult in the room. That doesn't mean its only job is to suck all the fun out (though unfortunately some people do that with their PFC). But it is there to regulate fun to make it safe, help create useful routines and boundaries, and get things back on track.

Don't make the mistake of thinking that the PFC is better than the other regions. All the parts of the brain must exist in a dynamic balance for you to have a happy and meaningful life. Too much regulation of your emotions can make you feel disconnected. Too little, and you're at their whims. Your emotions are like the stock market, and the prefrontal cortex offers responsible regulation. Too much unregulated enthusiasm leads to bubbles and hyperinflation. But on the other hand, too much fear can lead to recession.

Coloring

When I was in graduate school, one of our required textbooks was a coloring book. The distinguished professor knew that taking the time to color in the brain regions would help us commit them to memory. So if you've got some colored pencils lying around, or crayons, or different colored pens, then color in figures 1, 2, 3, and 4.

Chemicals of Depression

Your brain is composed of billions of tiny brain cells called *neurons*. Neurons are the basic units of processing in the brain. An individual brain cell sends out information via electrical transmission along thin tendrils that connect to other neurons. When an electrical signal reaches the end of a neuron, the neuron squirts out a chemical signal called a *neurotransmitter* to send information to the next neuron in the processing chain.

An individual neuron might connect to thousands of other neurons—some in the same brain region and others far away—creating vast networks, or systems, of neural communication. For example, neurons in the prefrontal cortex communicate with each other, and some communicate with the limbic system, and others communicate with the striatum, and neurons in those regions communicate with each other and with other regions and possibly even back to the prefrontal cortex.

There are dozens of different neurotransmitters operating within different neurotransmitter systems that influence each other. In addition, many other chemicals in the brain influence neuron communication and even neuron growth. Here is a table of the primary neurotransmitters and other chemicals involved in depression and overcoming it as well as a brief explanation of the functions to which they contribute. By utilizing the suggested interventions that you will read about in future chapters, you can actually modulate your brain chemistry, improving the function of these chemical systems to elevate your mood, increase resilience to stress and more.

Chemical	Function	Intervention
Serotonin	A neurotransmitter involved in willpower, controlling impulses, and regulating mood	Exercise (chapter 3), gratitude (chapter 10), sunlight (chapter 5)
Dopamine	A neurotransmitter involved in habits, impulses, addiction, and enjoyment	Enjoyable activities (chapter 2), exercise (chapter 3), gratitude (chapter 10), social connection (chapter 6)
Norepinephrine	A neurotransmitter involved in regulating stress	Exercise (chapter 3), sleep (chapter 5), increasing perceived control (chapter 7)
Oxytocin	A neurotransmitter and hormone involved in love and trust and human connection	Gratitude (chapter 10), physical touch (chapter 6), social support (chapter 6), music (chapter 4)
Endorphins	A group of neurotransmitters involved in euphoria and pain reduction	Exercise (chapter 3), stretching (chapter 4), massage and physical touch (chapter 6), social connection (chapter 6)
Endocannabinoids	A group of neurotransmitters involved in peacefulness and pain reduction	Exercise (chapter 3)
Melatonin	A hormone involved in quality sleep	Exercise (chapter 3), sunlight (chapter 5)

GABA	A neurotransmitter involved in reducing anxiety	Yoga (chapter 4)
BDNF	A brain chemical involved in strengthening neurons and growing new ones	Exercise (chapter 3)
Cortisol	A stress hormone—in general, lowering stress means reducing cortisol	Exercise (chapter 3), deep breathing (chapter 4), relaxing music (chapters 4), quality sleep (chapter 5), mindfulness (chapter 8)

Using Your Understanding of Neuroscience

While we haven't covered all the intricate complexities of the brain, we've covered enough to start making some helpful life changes. Here are a couple exercises that will allow you to apply your newfound knowledge.

Label Your Emotions

A lot of time, people, usually men (sorry guys), tell me that there's no point in discussing their feelings, because it amounts to wallowing in self-pity and won't solve anything. But neuroscience disagrees. A cool set of studies conducted at UCLA shows that simply by labeling the emotion you're feeling, your prefrontal cortex can soothe your amygdala's emotional response (Lieberman et al., 2007).

What follows is a list of some common emotions (and variants) in depression and anxiety. Circle any emotions that you're feeling right now. Add your own, or any that are missing, by writing in the blank spaces. Put a check next to emotions that you feel are particularly relevant to you, so the next time they pop up, you can identify them more readily.

☐ **Sad**	☐ Frozen	☐ Deserted	☐ Empty
☐ Dejected	☐ Hesitant	☐ Friendless	☐ Exhausted
☐ Down	☐ Jittery	☐ Isolated	☐ Sleepy
☐ Depressed	☐ Nervous	☐ Lonely	☐ Tired
☐ Gloomy	☐ Overwhelmed	☐ Rejected	☐ Weary
☐ Heartbroken	☐ Panicked	☐ **Guilty**	☐ **Angry**
☐ Melancholy	☐ Scared	☐ Ashamed	☐ Furious
☐ Miserable	☐ Stressed	☐ Regretful	☐ Irritable
☐ Unhappy	☐ Terrified	☐ Sorry	☐ Mad
☐ **Anxious**	☐ Uneasy	☐ Worthless	☐ Steaming
☐ Agitated	☐ Worried	☐ **Fatigued**	☐ _____
☐ Apprehensive	☐ **Alone**	☐ Drowsy	☐ _____
☐ Concerned	☐ Abandoned	☐ Drained	☐ _____

Emotions and the body's physiology are intertwined, and thus there is a strong connection between depression and physical symptoms. For example, physical pain and depression are closely linked, particularly for back pain and headaches. Because chronic pain increases risk for depression, and depression increases risk for chronic pain, it's an unfortunate downward spiral. The same can be true for breathing difficulties, as they disrupt the body's ability to calm the brain (chapter 4).

There is also a strong connection between the limbic system and the digestive system. For example, when I was a kid, I never would have said I had a lot of anxiety, I just got stomachaches when I had a test coming up or if I was waiting in line for a roller coaster that I didn't want to go on.

Physical symptoms can be related to mood and anxiety. Pain and suffering are not just a result of pain signals coming from the body but also how those signals are processed by the brain. For example, communication between the insula and the limbic system correlates with anxiety (Baur,

Hänggi, Langer, & Jäncke, 2013). In addition, people suffering from either depression or chronic pain have altered communication between the insula and the limbic system (Ichesco et al., 2012; Avery et al., 2014). That means the brain is sensitized to feel more pain and have a stronger emotional reaction to it—an unfortunate combination.

Recognizing Physical Symptoms

Recognizing that your physical symptoms are related to mood and anxiety can be very helpful. It does not make them go away, but it's a first step in regulating the communication between the prefrontal cortex, limbic system, and insula.

Look at the list below, and circle any physical sensations you're feeling right now. Put a check next to any that you commonly feel. Write in any others that come to mind.

- ☐ Backache
- ☐ Butterflies in your stomach
- ☐ Chest pains
- ☐ Clenching or grinding teeth
- ☐ Cramps
- ☐ Difficulty breathing
- ☐ Difficulty sleeping
- ☐ Dizzy or light-headed

- ☐ Dry mouth
- ☐ Feeling numb or tingly
- ☐ Frequent colds or other illnesses
- ☐ Goosebumps
- ☐ Headache
- ☐ Heartburn or indigestion
- ☐ Jaw pain
- ☐ Nausea
- ☐ Neck pain

- ☐ Pounding or racing heart
- ☐ Shaky hands
- ☐ Stomachache
- ☐ Tense muscles
- ☐ Sweating
- ☐ Weakness
- ☐ _____
- ☐ _____
- ☐ _____
- ☐ _____

Relevance of the Neurobiology

When suffering from depression, it's easy to feel like you're broken. But that's where understanding different brain regions can be so powerful.

If you were to break your arm, you might say that your arm is broken, but you would not say that *you* were broken. It's easy to see that your arm is not you. You can hold it up and wiggle the fingers. It's part of you or something you possess, but it is not you.

But when you feel sad, or hopeless, or anxious, it is hard to see these things as being separate from you. But they are. They are how you're experiencing the world at the moment. These thoughts and feelings originate from specific brain regions that you possess. You are not your amygdala. You are not your hypothalamus. You possess them, and they may cause you problems at times, but they are not who you are.

People are often looking to fix their emotions. But emotions aren't something you can fix, because they're not broken. They are simply a result of your various brain regions doing what they evolved to do.

Now that you know the various brain regions and chemicals, take a moment to reflect on each and how they might be relevant to your current situation. You can write down your thoughts in the space below. If you don't see any of them as relevant, no worries, this is just the beginning.

_____

_____

_____

_____

_____

What You Can't Control—And What You Can

Psychologist Sonja Lyubomirsky (2008) studies happiness, and her research has found just how much control people have over their own happiness. Some of it is beyond your control, caused by your genes, your early childhood experiences, and other aspects of your life that you can't change. But a full 40 percent is within your control.

If 40 percent sounds unfortunately low (I mean, it's not even half), you're not wrong, per se, but that characterization isn't helpful. In fact, that kind of automatic negative focus of your brain is likely contributing to a downward spiral.

Forty percent is actually quite a lot, if you think about it. In terms of academic grades, 40 percent is the difference between getting an F and an A. Hardly any other feature about yourself can be changed by that much. You can't get 40 percent taller or 40 percent smarter. So if you feel like you're failing the happiness test, there's hope. And this book is here to help.

While it may feel sometimes like you're the only one suffering, and that everyone else is just carried through their day on sunshine and rainbows, depression and anxiety are very common. Every year, tens of millions of Americans suffer from one or both. You just don't realize it, because most people don't talk about depression or what they're doing to take care of themselves. Other than Instagramming a pampering day at the spa, self-care isn't something we really advertise, at least not when it comes to the rough-and-tumble world of depression and anxiety. No one posts pictures of themselves successfully getting out of bed to brush their teeth. You don't really know what other people are going through or how they're coping.

You are not alone. It just feels that way. That's a symptom of depression.

Depression is so common because the same brain circuits that make us human also have this unfortunate tendency to sometimes get stuck in a pattern of depression. That means there are some aspects of your condition—and your brain—that you may not be able to change. The activity and chemistry of your various brain circuits are shaped by many forces, some of which are under your control and some of which aren't. It's important to understand that you don't have total control over your biology.

This may sound like a strange goal for a self-help book, but, in fact, accepting your limitations frees you to focus on those aspects of your life and brain that you *can* change. This chapter is an important starting point, because until you accept where you are, it is difficult to move forward.

How Did Your Brain Get This Way?

It starts with genetics, the specific genes that your parents passed down to you. Certain genes increase the risk for depression, because they start to shape the tuning of specific emotional circuits. But genes are not destiny. They just create a propensity for your neural circuits to develop in a particular way.

The next big factor is your early childhood experiences, particularly any trauma you encountered. These experiences have a big effect on how various brain circuits develop and how your genes get expressed—a process influenced by something called *epigenetics*. Epigenetics can activate or deactivate certain genes, turning them up or quieting them down (Miller, 2017). Sometimes these developments are helpful, sometimes less so. Are there any particular childhood experiences that you feel are pushing your brain toward depression? Writing about difficult experiences in detail has many benefits (chapter 5), but for now, you can just list some that come to mind.

_____

_____

_____

_____

_____

You can't change your genes, but that's okay—you don't have to change them to overcome depression. In fact, making small changes in your thoughts and actions can influence your epigenetics, making it possible to turn up or turn down the influence of your genes.

While you also can't change your early childhood experiences, you can sometimes reframe them from a different perspective and change your beliefs about them, which will have a positive impact on your brain. Epigenetic mechanisms and beliefs about your past experiences are both happening in the present, which brings us to the last piece of the puzzle: current life circumstances.

Reviewing Your Current Life Circumstances

Your current life circumstances include your work (or lack thereof), relationships, coping habits, attitude, beliefs, exercise, sleep, and recent experiences. Do you think any of these are contributing to your depression? Explain.

Relationships: _____

_____

Coping habits: _____

_____

Attitude: _____

_____

Beliefs: _____

_____

Exercise: _____

_____

Sleep: _____

_____

Recent experiences: _____

_____

Other experiences: _____

_____

The purpose of this exercise is to understand the factors influencing your brain activity and chemistry. Your current life circumstances are the only piece of the puzzle that you have some control over, though not total control. Some of those factors you may be able to change, and some you may not—and often it's not obvious which category these factors fall into.

Knowing where you are now will help you figure out what areas to address in future chapters. The path forward will include a mix of changing some of the life circumstances that you can control and learning to accept others that you can't.

Understanding Your Own Goals

What are you looking for that made you pick up this book? What do you hope to achieve? Take five minutes to write down what you'd like to get out of this book. It's okay if you don't even fully understand—just write down that you're not sure. The process of finding a way forward is not a straight line—you might even call it a spiral—so we'll revisit this again later (chapter 7). But doing something and getting it wrong, and doing it again and still getting it not quite right, is much more useful than never doing anything at all.

_____

_____

_____

_____

_____

_____

_____

Is Something Wrong With Your Brain?

When people find out that I study depression and have access to an MRI machine, they often ask me, "So, what's wrong with my brain?" The answer usually surprises them: "Nothing."

When you're in the depths of despair and darkness or overwhelmed by roiling anxiety, it feels like something is very wrong with your brain. But that's just how it feels, not how it actually is. Your brain can get stuck in unhelpful patterns of activity and reactivity, even though there's nothing wrong with it.

What? Isn't half this chapter about problematic brain regions? Aren't there tons of studies about brain regions being altered in depression? Sure, if you take twenty people with depression and twenty people without it and scan their brains while they are in a lab doing a specific task, you can find average differences in activity in specific brain regions. But those differences are *on average*. They are small statistical deviations. You can't look at someone's brain and know if they're depressed or not. No brain scan or lab test can diagnose someone with depression. But how can you get a disorder like depression without something being wrong with the brain?

As I described in *The Upward Spiral,* to understand the circuitry of your brain, think of a simple feedback circuit like a microphone and a speaker. If the microphone is oriented in just a particular way and the volume on the speaker is turned up just a little too high, then even a soft sound can lead to screeching feedback. There's nothing wrong with the microphone and nothing wrong with the speaker. Both are working exactly as they're supposed to. The problem arises from the system: the communication between the parts and the inputs that they get.

The same is true of your brain. Nothing is wrong with your amygdala or prefrontal cortex or anything else. They're all working as they're supposed to. The reason you're stuck is because of the dynamics of how they're communicating and the inputs that they receive, such as your social inter-actions and your environment.

Fortunately, solving the microphone problem doesn't require replacing the microphone or the speaker; you can just reorient the microphone or turn down the volume on the speaker. Even though your brain is much more complex, it's helpful to think about your neural circuits similarly when you're doing the various interventions in this book. Some interventions help turn down the volume on your anxiety circuit. In other cases, you're turning up the volume on your motivation or decision-making circuit.

You can also think of your brain like a guitar. Whether you got it new from a careful craftsman or from the five-and-dime, it's still capable of creating beautiful music. But even if it's well made, the guitar will sound awful if it's out of tune. There's nothing wrong with it—some strings are just a little flat or a little sharp. This book will help you get your brain back in tune.

What I hope you get from this particular chapter is this. (1) There's nothing wrong with you. (2) When you're depressed, your brain tends to think and act in ways that keep you depressed, so it won't always be easy to change. (3) You can make small but meaningful and powerful changes to positively impact your mood and well-being.

You Are Not to Blame

Notice if you start to blame yourself or put yourself down for feeling depressed. Being depressed is not your fault. It's not even your brain's fault. There is no fault—only numerous contributing factors. It's just like other medical conditions, such as diabetes or heart disease.

If someone develops diabetes or heart problems, it's not their fault: it's their biology. Some unhelpful life decisions may have contributed to their condition, but it's still not their fault. However, by making small changes in their diet, exercise, and stress levels, they can positively impact their condition. The same is true of depression.

It is not your fault, but you can be part of the solution. There is hope for change. How does that new way of thinking feel?

_____

_____

_____

_____

_____

Moving Forward and Upward

While this chapter has been focused on understanding your brain, the rest of the book is focused on small life changes you can make that will positively impact your brain's activity and chemistry. Each small change may not be the solution, but each contributes to improvement—a part of the upward spiral. While there are no guarantees, accepting uncertainty is itself part of the way up (see chapter 7). Each small change stacks the deck in your favor. But understanding is just the beginning.

A few years ago, I went to a motivational workshop looking for a boost. The speaker talked about many ways of reframing situations and about things you could do to get out of a funk. It wasn't making sense to me, so I asked for clarification: "I see what you're suggesting, but I don't understand how that's going to help."

He replied, "You're trying too hard to understand. Just do it."

While understanding is helpful, it is not the whole answer. Understanding can be very powerful if it leads to action or acceptance, but in trying to understand, it is easy to overthink things.

The activities in this book will work whether you understand the neuroscience or not. So if you get stuck on trying to understand, stop worrying about it. The main purpose of the neuroscience is to help you move forward into action.

Now you've got a better picture of what's going on in the brain and hopefully some inklings of how the chemistry and activity of key brain circuits can be modulated. As we progress into various realms of life changes, keep trying to put things in terms that you can understand, but don't let a question of understanding be a barrier. Use your understanding of neuroscience to keep moving forward and upward.

Chapter 2

The Activity Spiral

Karma is an important element of the Hindu tradition—it adds up over the course of many lives, with good deeds leading to good consequences and bad deeds leading to bad consequences. Karma is also an important part of this book, and the focus of this chapter. But wait, isn't this book about neuroscience? Yes. Be patient—it's good karma.

In Sanskrit, the word *karma* translates literally to "action." So this chapter is about karma, not in some cosmic sense but just literally in the sense that actions have consequences. Your actions, whether intentional or unintentional, have consequences for the activity and chemistry of key neural circuits. A fact that you can take advantage of to create an upward spiral.

This idea is exploited by one of the most effective treatments for depression: behavioral activation therapy. *Behavioral activation* focuses on changing unhelpful behaviors that contribute to depression and incorporating more helpful ones. This type of approach has been shown to alter the activity in the emotion regulation, motivation, and habit circuits in the brain—the medial prefrontal cortex, orbitofrontal cortex, and dorsal striatum, respectively (Dichter et al., 2009).

The good news is that this isn't the kind of book where I say you have to do everything you hate. Behavioral activation therapy is just a fancy way of saying "start doing stuff." Incorporate more positive activities in your life—enjoyable activities, meaningful activities, and activities that provide a sense of progress. While it might seem too simple, these activities have measurable and meaningful consequences for your brain activity and chemistry. In other words: good karma.

What to Do

To reverse the course of depression, there are five main types of activities that are helpful to do more of:

- Enjoyable activities—activities that are fun, rewarding, calming, exciting, or even ones that simply sustain your attention

- Achievement activities—activities where you get better at something or complete something, contributing to a sense of mastery or accomplishment.

- Meaningful activities—activities that create a greater sense of purpose or create a connection to other people or to ideas larger than yourself

- Physical activities—activities that get your body moving, like hiking, biking, or playing sports

- Social activities—activities done with other people

While there is a lot of overlap in these types of activities (for example, many meaningful activities like a family vacation are also social), that's good news—a two-for-one deal! And perhaps you already do some of these types of activities. Great—now you can count them as part of your getting better. Another two-for-one deal.

These types of activities are so beneficial because you can lose yourself in the activity and not lose yourself in your negative thoughts. This chapter will focus on enjoyable, achievement, and meaningful activities. Chapters 3 and 4 focus on physical activities, and chapter 6 focuses on social activities.

Choosing Activities

Are you more active when you're not depressed? Think back to times when you were not depressed. What activities did you engage in? Can you start doing any of those activities again? Don't worry if you don't feel like it—when you're depressed, if you only do things you feel like, then you end up staying depressed. So you just need to start doing things. This table has some suggestions. Of course, I don't know what you like to do, or what you find meaningful, so fill in the blank spaces with your own favorite activities.

Enjoyable Activities	Achievement Activities	Meaningful Activities
Taking a bath	Doing a crossword puzzle	Spending time with family
Watching sports	Washing dishes	Going to church or participating in religious activities
Playing sports	Doing laundry	Watching your favorite sports team
Gardening	Paying bills	Spending time with a good friend
Reading a book	Reading a book	Reading a book
Eating	Engaging in hobbies	Visiting a museum or art gallery
Cooking	Planning a vacation	Checking an item off your bucket list
Playing music	Going to the gym	Making a gift for someone
Drawing or other arts	Fixing things	Writing in a journal
Driving	Practicing a musical instrument	Writing a short story or screenplay
Going to concerts or plays	Going for a walk, hike, or run	Joining a local sports league
Watching TV and movies	Learning a new language	Volunteering at a local charity
Taking a trip	Taking a dance class	
	Taking a woodworking class	
	Taking a cooking class	

What are some activities you used to do before you got depressed?

_____

_____

_____

_____

What are some activities you enjoy, but don't do as much as you'd like?

_____

_____

_____

_____

What are some activities that you're good at, or that help you feel competent and successful?

_____

_____

_____

_____

Even though it may feel difficult and pointless to engage in these types of activities, that will change over time. With repetition, you can train a habit into your striatum to make things easier. Repetition also helps make activities more meaningful, particularly if you involve other people. But the first step is to start.

Scheduling Activities

Your intention to do these activities is not what will get you better, nor will understanding their importance help get you better. When it comes to activities, it's not the thought that counts. It's the *doing*.

To facilitate actually doing more positive activities, it's important to plan them into your schedule. As soon as you put an activity on your calendar, it starts to become real. And the brain treats real things and imaginary things differently. Imaginary things require more willpower and prefrontal involvement, but the more real and concrete something is, the more the striatum is involved—allowing you to accomplish it with less willpower.

Here's a calendar for the week. First, write in the times you plan on sleeping. This is a great way to organize the day. Remember that by sleeping you're not wasting time—you're actually accomplishing something that will help with your depression (more on this in chapter 5). So, write SLEEP in big capital letters.

Then write down the other activities that fill your day, like work and meals. Add in some of the enjoyable, achievement-oriented, or meaningful activities that you identified in the previous exercise. Start small, so you don't feel overwhelmed, and actually do the things you write down.

You can visit http://www.newharbinger.com/42426 to download this activity-scheduling calendar, or you can use your own day planner or the calendar on your smartphone. Physically writing down your plans has the benefit of making them feel more tangible, though electronic calendars have the benefit of sending reminders. Fill out this activity-scheduling calendar for at least one week, but then you can choose whichever calendar you prefer.

Activity-Scheduling Calendar

Time	Mon.	Tue.	Wed.	Thu.	Fri.	Sat.	Sun.
12:00 a.m.							
1:00 a.m.							
2:00 a.m.							
3:00 a.m.							
4:00 a.m.							
5:00 a.m.							
6:00 a.m.							
7:00 a.m.							
8:00 a.m.							
9:00 a.m.							
10:00 a.m.							

11:00 a.m.	12:00 p.m.	1:00 p.m.	2:00 p.m.	3:00 p.m.	4:00 p.m.	5:00 p.m.	6:00 p.m.	7:00 p.m.	8:00 p.m.	9:00 p.m.	10:00 p.m.	11:00 p.m.

Identifying Unhelpful Thoughts

While you're thinking about helpful activities, unhelpful thoughts may pop into your head that threaten to disrupt your plans. Unhelpful thoughts are simply ones that make it feel harder to do helpful activities. These thoughts can trigger anxieties and get your mind racing from one worry to another or orbiting around the same worry over and over.

Patterns of unhelpful thoughts are common in depression. They are a result of the activity in your limbic system and striatum.

Fortunately, to engage in helpful activities, you don't need to eliminate unhelpful thoughts. In fact, you can't control which thoughts pop into your head—trying to control them will be frustrating and stressful (and focusing on what you can't control elevates limbic reactivity).

The first thing to acknowledge is that your thoughts are not *the truth*! They may be related to the truth, or contain elements of truth, but they are triggered, filtered, and distorted by your neural circuitry. For example, take the thought that a *meteor could land on my house and kill me*. That's technically true, but it's so unlikely that it's not at all relevant.

It's not the thoughts that matter. It's what you do with the thoughts that matters. If you're trying to enjoy time with your family, and a thought pops into your head like *I should be getting work done*, is that a helpful or unhelpful thought? It's helpful if it inspires you to work harder once you're back at the office, or even if it causes you to realize that you would prefer to be working instead of being with your family. But it's unhelpful if it diminishes your current enjoyment or results in demoralizing self-criticism. You can't choose the thoughts that pop into your head, but you can choose what you do with those thoughts.

Your thoughts may affect your actions, behaviors, interactions, physiology, and emotions, but they are not the same thing as feelings or actions. It sounds silly written down, but it's harder to appreciate when you're living it, because unhelpful thoughts are often automatic and quickly followed by strong emotions or urges to act. But your thoughts are just thoughts—the whisperings of your limbic system and your striatum.

Thoughts are something you have, but they are not who you are. You are not your limbic system. You are not your striatum.

Identifying, acknowledging, and reframing unhelpful thoughts will be something we'll revisit throughout this book. Taking these small steps helps the prefrontal cortex get a runaway limbic system back under control (Ochsner et al., 2004)

When you notice an unhelpful thought getting in the way of creating an upward spiral, it can be helpful to challenge it or argue with it, just as you might argue with another person. But just like with people, sometimes your thoughts don't listen to reason, and they keep pestering you. In that case, it can often be helpful to just ignore them and go on about your day.

Here are a few common unhelpful thought patterns, so you can more readily identify them.

Black-or-White Thinking

Black-or-white thinking involves creating arbitrary dichotomous categories, such as labeling things as either good or bad. For example, *I will either love this or hate it.*

Challenging black-or-white thinking: Life does not fall neatly into clean categories. There are many shades of gray and a whole rainbow of colors. There are usually some good and bad aspects to everything. Allow some space for nuance.

Unrealistic Expectations

Rather than basing our life satisfaction on the good things that happen to us, we base it on the difference between what happens and what we thought would happen. So, having unrealistic expectations is problematic. For example, *Once I start doing helpful activities, my depression will improve right away.*

Challenging unrealistic expectations: Ask yourself if your expectations are realistic, or if your high expectations are getting in the way of your happiness. The reality is that helpful activities do facilitate an upward spiral, though that doesn't mean you should expect a quick and easy recovery. But even though it might be difficult to move forward, it's important to you—otherwise you wouldn't be reading this book.

Selective Attention

Selective attention becomes a problem when we pay particular attention to the negative aspects of a situation rather than the positive ones. It also includes paying more attention to negative events and ignoring or minimizing positive events. Examples include *There are so many things I have to do or my depression will get worse* or *Changing my activities never improves my mood.*

Challenging selective attention: First, when you use the words "have to," you're framing activities as responsibilities rather than things you might actually enjoy. And often the things we have to do and the things we want to do are the same things. Focusing on the fact that you want to do them makes them more fun and rewarding. Second, when you focus on potential negative consequences rather than potential positive consequences, it increases stress. It would be more helpful to say "There are so many things I could do to help myself feel better."

In addition, any time you notice yourself saying "never" or "always," pause for a moment and think of counterexamples. When you find counterexamples, you may be tempted to dismiss them as irrelevant, but that's another type of cognitive distortion known as *disqualifying the positive.*

Disqualifying the Positive

This means to dismiss certain examples or experiences because they "don't count" for some reason. For example, *I felt better after that one time I went to a party, but that was just a fluke.*

Challenging disqualifying the positive: Make a conscious decision to count all positive experiences, no matter how unlikely or isolated they seem.

Predicting the Future

Your brain makes lots of predictions about the future. That's one of the features of the prefrontal cortex. But when you're depressed, those predictions are often skewed negative. For example, *It's not really going to help much, so there's no point in trying.*

Challenging predicting the future: Acknowledge that you really don't know what's going to happen in the future, and neither does anyone else. Ask yourself whether your prediction about the future will help you take potentially positive actions or if it is just getting in the way.

Recognizing Unhelpful Thoughts

What are some unhelpful thoughts you have that get in the way of doing activities or make them seem less appealing? Do you notice any unhelpful thought patterns? Do you see other patterns besides those listed in this chapter?

_____

_____

_____

_____

_____

You don't need to categorize them correctly—in fact, these patterns overlap a lot. You don't even need to try to categorize them at all. Just recognizing certain thoughts as unhelpful is all that's needed to start moving forward.

Barriers to Activities

When you're depressed, it's easy to judge yourself for not doing something that seems easy. But usually when you don't do something that you think you want to do, your brain has a good reason for it—or at least a reason. You may not like the reason, but identifying the reason can help reduce self-judgment and offer a path forward.

A myriad of barriers can get in the way of doing positive activities. Here's a list of some common barriers along with some suggested strategies to find a way forward. Check off any that you feel are impeding your ability to engage in helpful activities. If you can do something to overcome a particular barrier, then check off one of the suggested solutions or write down one small step you can take to move forward. If you can't do anything about it, then the only way forward is to accept it as a limitation (more on this in chapter 8). Once you accept your limitations, then they stop being so limiting, because acceptance frees you up to focus on the things that you can actually do something about.

☐ *I have an injury, or it would be too painful.*

    ☐ List some easier activities that you find manageable and start with those.

    ☐ Go see a doctor, physical therapist, or other health professional, and get help for existing injuries/illnesses.

    ☐ _____

    ☐ Accept this as a limitation.

☐ *It takes too much time.*

    ☐ Manage your time more efficiently by using a calendar.

    ☐ Prioritize brief sessions of helpful activities over less important ones.

    ☐ Start with really small changes (such as five minutes a day).

    ☐ Integrate activities into things you already have to do (for example, if you're meeting a friend for coffee, ask if you can take a walk together instead).

    ☐ _____

    ☐ Accept this as a limitation.

☐ *It takes too much money.*

    ☐ Find activities that are free or basically free, such as hiking, listening to podcasts, or hanging out with friends.

    ☐ Take stock of what you're spending your money on. Is it on things that are important to you or that bring you happiness? If so, great, you're prioritizing your budget on things that are important. If not, great. This is an opportunity to reallocate your funds.

    ☐ _____

    ☐ Accept this as a limitation.

☐ *It takes too much energy.*

    ☐ Improve your sleep (chapter 5). Quality sleep gives you more energy to be active, and being active improves the quality of your sleep: a beautiful upward spiral!

    ☐ Make it a habit! The more you repeat an activity, the more it gets ingrained in the dorsal striatum, and the less willpower and energy it requires (chapter 9).

    ☐ Do the activity with other people (chapter 6). You can benefit from their energy and enthusiasm.

    ☐ _____

    ☐ Accept this as a limitation.

☐ *I don't feel like it.*

    ☐ Just do it. You don't need to feel like doing an activity in order to do it. Don't focus on changing your feelings to start—it's an unnecessary barrier. Just change your actions.

    ☐ Change your environment or context. Your mood, energy levels, decisions, and habits are affected by your surroundings. Instead of trying to work up the willpower to do something, simply go where it's easier to do it, or take steps that move you in that direction. Don't feel like being productive at home? Leave your house. Don't feel like going to a party? First get dressed. Don't feel like exercising? Drive to the gym, and then make the decision from there. You don't know how you really feel until you change your surroundings.

☐ Recognizing and labeling your negative feelings helps the prefrontal cortex regulate the emotional limbic system, providing an opportunity to act intentionally rather than reactively.

☐ _____

☐ Accept this as a limitation.

What are your limitations? And given your limitations, what is possible?

_____

_____

_____

_____

_____

_____

_____

Conclusion

Depression is a complex disorder, but sometimes the solutions are simple—like doing activities that you enjoy or that create a sense of progress. But, then again, while these activities may seem simple, they actually have a lot of complex neuroscience behind them, and they are a powerful way to create and sustain an upward spiral.

Chapter 3

The Movement Spiral

The founding director of the National Institute on Aging, Dr. Robert Butler, devoted his scientific career to understanding how to keep the brain and body healthy long into old age. After years of research, he famously declared, "If exercise could be packed into a pill, it would be the single most widely prescribed and beneficial medicine in the nation" (Butler, 1978, p. 193). And while many pills have been developed in the intervening years, none have quite matched the robust and nuanced effects that exercise has on the brain and the neural circuits of depression and anxiety.

This chapter and the next both focus on the relationship between the brain and the body. This chapter focuses on moving your body and the many positive influences that physical activity has on mood, anxiety, stress, and energy levels as it targets key brain regions and neurotransmitters. Many of these types of movement could be described as "exercise," but that word sometimes sucks all the enjoyment out of it.

Getting your body moving is often the most straightforward way to start reversing the course of depression. It's sometimes harder to be mindful of your thoughts or to recognize bad habits, but physical activity is easy to understand (although that doesn't mean it's always easy to do). To facilitate getting moving, we'll start with some of the benefits to you and your brain.

Benefits of Physical Activity

The human brain evolved on the open savannahs of East Africa when the human body tended to be a lot more active than it is in the modern era. Early humans never thought about going to the gym or taking a spin class; their lifestyles simply required more physical activity. Just as wild animals don't do well in captivity, your brain does not do as well when your butt is glued to a chair all day.

Dozens of studies have shown that exercise helps with depression overall, along with many specific symptoms of depression. It can improve mood, focus, and energy levels and reduce physical pain and stress. Exercise can have so many effects because it impacts so many different brain regions and neurotransmitter systems.

Keeping the brain in mind is helpful, because there are definitely times, particularly if you're out of shape, when exercise feels crappy. Fortunately, with repetition, it will potentially even start to feel good at times. But regardless of how it makes you feel at the moment, it's still providing important and lasting changes to your brain.

Considering the Benefits

Check off any benefits of physical activity that are particularly important to you.

Physical activity...

☐ Improves willpower and regulates mood

Physical activity boosts the neurotransmitter serotonin (Melancon, Lorrain, & Dionne, 2014). This helps strengthen the prefrontal cortex and its ability to regulate mood.

☐ Reduces stress and its harmful effects

Over time, exercise reduces the stress hormone cortisol (Nabkasorn et al., 2006). Interestingly, exercise itself is a form of stress, but it's good stress, because you're choosing to do it. Exercise also enhances the brain's release of a chemical called *brain-derived neurotrophic factor* (BDNF), which is like fertilizer for your brain. BDNF makes neurons more resilient to stress and even helps grow new neurons in the hippocampus (Olson, Eadie, Ernst, & Christie, 2006).

☐ Supports healthy habits

Do you find yourself being impulsive and unable to overcome your bad habits? Exercise can help with that by modifying the striatum circuits that control habits (Janse Van Rensburg, Taylor, Hodgson, & Benattayallah, 2009). The neurotransmitter dopamine is particularly important in these circuits.

☐ Enhances enjoyment

Repeated exercise creates more dopamine receptors in the nucleus accumbens (Greenwood et al., 2011). These effects on the dopamine system explain why exercise helps increase enjoyment and pleasure, and not just enjoyment of exercise but pleasure in other areas of your life as well.

☐ Decreases pain and discomfort

Aches and pains got you down? Exercise can help. Two chemicals in particular play an important role: endorphins (Boecker et al., 2008) and endocannabinoids (Sparling, Giuffrida, Piomelli, Rosskopf, & Dietrich, 2003). Endorphins are the brain's own form of morphine, while endocannabinoids are the brain's own form of cannabis (i.e., marijuana). These chemicals help reduce pain and enhance well-being and joy. This highlights an important point: any drug that has an effect on the brain only works because the brain is capable of producing a chemical that does the same thing. When you take it externally, it goes everywhere in the brain and can have unintended negative consequences. But getting the brain to produce the chemicals on its own allows them to work in more targeted and nuanced ways.

☐ Improves sleep quality

Do you have insomnia or other problems with sleep? As you'll find in chapter 5, exercise can make it easier to fall asleep, particularly early evening exercise (Buxton, Lee, L'Hermite-Baleriaux, Turek, & Van Cauter, 2003). It improves sleep quality as well by altering the electrical activity of the brain during sleep to make it more restful.

Even just thinking about how you can benefit from exercise helps the prefrontal cortex modulate enjoyment in the nucleus accumbens. What benefits do you envision with exercising more?

_____

_____

_____

Just Do It

How do you start exercising? Well, the iconic Nike ad campaign got one important thing right: there's no way to do something other than to just do it. To illustrate, think about moving your arm. Desire to move your arm. Plan to move your arm. Now, move your arm.

The plans and the desires to move are not necessary parts of moving. They utilize prefrontal or limbic regions but are not necessary to actually move. There is no way to think yourself into moving or to feel your way into moving. You just have to do it.

The small amount of exercise you actually do is infinitely more beneficial than the large amount of exercise you plan to do but don't end up doing. With that in mind, let's get moving.

After this paragraph, stop reading. Just for a moment. Stand up and walk around the room. Do ten jumping jacks, or if you can't do that, try shadow boxing (punching the air lightly) for fifteen seconds. Now stop reading. I'll wait.

I'm not joking—if you haven't moved your body, then this chapter can't help you. Take a moment and move your body. Trust me; the rest of the chapter will be here when you get back.

...

Do you notice any difference in how your body feels or differences in your mood, energy, or stress levels? Please describe:

_____

_____

_____

_____

_____

_____

That small amount of exercise is already setting you on the right track. Even brief repetitive movements start to modify the serotonin system (Jacobs & Fornal, 1999). Each time you do something, stronger connections get created in the striatum to make it easier to do again. This is sometimes called *muscle memory*, but it's not actually in your muscles; it's in your brain. It's just that you have to do the action to take advantage of this.

Just Get Moving

What do you picture when you hear the word "exercise"? I think of a hot, sweaty gym with rows and rows of people on treadmills, ellipticals, and StairMasters, all wearing headphones or blankly staring at TV sets tuned to CNN. This chapter is called "The Movement Spiral," and not "The Exercise Spiral," for a reason—mainly that exercise sounds like something your doctor said you needed to do for your health or like a lame activity you were forced to do in middle-school gym class.

Thinking of movement and activities as something you're supposed to do—or should do or have to do—usually isn't helpful. Once you stop thinking about what you're supposed to do, it's easier to uncover what you want to do, and often they're the same thing. If thinking *it's exercise* makes the activity tougher to enjoy, then just think of it as physical activity or movement.

Physical activity doesn't have to be difficult or boring. It can be fun. It is an opportunity to enjoy your body—an opportunity to breathe deep and engage with the world. The simple act of moving can have profound consequences. It is willful. It is physical. It is emotional and potentially even spiritual.

Think back to the previous chapter. Were there any enjoyable or meaningful activities or things you're good at that you could do that also involve physical activity? Or can you think of any new ones? If so, write them down, and if not, see the list in this next exercise.

_____

_____

_____

Move Your Body

Step 1. Look down at the list of physical activity suggestions, and circle the activities that you have an interest in doing. If there are other exercises that come to mind, then write them in the blank spaces provided.

Step 2. After you go through the list once, then go through it again and check off each item that you're capable of doing—even if it's inconvenient or unlikely. You can worry about the practicalities later.

Step 3. Put a star next to one exercise that pushes your comfort level ever so slightly. So if you're finding it difficult to get up off the couch, then put a star next to "walking around the house." If walking around the block seems easy, then put a star next to something more difficult like "jumping jacks" or "yoga."

Step 4. If you can do your starred exercise right now, then do it right now. Maybe that just means a two-minute jog or five jumping jacks or one push-up. Otherwise, make a plan to do your starred exercise. Once you complete it, then put a check next to your star. That's it. Congratulations! Later on we'll explore how to keep the exercise spiral going, but the good news is that it has already begun.

Physical Activity Suggestions

☐ Getting up off the couch

☐ Walking around the house

☐ Walking around the block

☐ Running errands (the mall, the supermarket, etc.)

☐ Yard work (raking leaves, shoveling snow, etc.)

☐ Walking in the park

☐ Walking up and down stairs

☐ Playing catch (football, baseball, Frisbee)

☐ Hitting golf balls at driving range

☐ Doing push-ups, sit-ups, deep knee bends or lunges

☐ Doing planks/side planks

☐ Jumping (such as jumping jacks)

☐ Practicing tai chi

☐ Curling

☐ Hiking

☐ Playing active video games (Wii Fit)

☐ Dancing (with yourself, at a dance class, or at the club)

☐ Shooting hoops

☐ Hitting balls at a batting cage

☐ Bowling

☐ Horseback riding

☐ Climbing stairs

☐ Using an elliptical machine

☐ Swimming

☐ Jogging

☐ Biking (outside, stationary, or spin class)

☐ Rowing (on the river or on a machine)

☐ Practicing yoga

☐ Doing Pilates

☐ Doing capoeira

☐ Hula hooping

☐ Skateboarding, scooting, or skating (roller or ice)

☐ Surfing (waves, not the web)

☐ Canoeing/kayaking

☐ Paddleboarding

☐ Taking a cardio class

☐ Shadowboxing

☐ Jumping rope

☐ Cardio kickboxing

☐ Weight lifting

- ☐ Rock climbing
- ☐ Playing sports:
    - ☐ Baseball/softball/kickball
    - ☐ Dodgeball
    - ☐ Tennis (on the court or on a table)
    - ☐ Golf (regular, mini, or Frisbee)
    - ☐ Volleyball
    - ☐ Basketball
    - ☐ Ultimate Frisbee
    - ☐ Football/flag football
    - ☐ Racquetball
    - ☐ Squash
    - ☐ Soccer
    - ☐ Hockey
- ☐ Lacrosse
- ☐ Running a 5K/10K/marathon
- ☐ Training for a triathlon
- ☐ Boxing/martial arts
- ☐ Doing CrossFit
- ☐ _____
- ☐ _____
- ☐ _____
- ☐ _____
- ☐ _____
- ☐ _____
- ☐ _____

The Specifics

If you're the type of person who just wants me to cut to the chase and tell you what to do, you're in luck. I'm going to present some recommendations for physical exercise that scientists and doctors have determined work on average for alleviating depression. But before I do, you have to promise to use these as guidelines rather than see them as a requirement. It might sound like a lot, and if you're going to find that disheartening, just skip to the next section and don't worry about this for now.

The guidelines to achieving the maximum antidepressant effect of exercise is three to five sessions per week of moderate intensity exercise for forty-five to sixty minutes (Rethorst & Trivedi, 2013). Keep it up for at least ten weeks to get the maximum antidepressant effect.

Studies show that the type of exercise doesn't matter much, just so long as you do it regularly. It could be aerobic exercise like brisk walking, running, cycling, or playing sports, or it could be strengthening exercises like weightlifting, Pilates, or yoga. Strengthening exercises should include both upper and lower body.

So go for a jog or a bike ride or head to the gym and pick your favorite aerobic machine. Do a slow five-minute warm-up, and then thirty minutes of moderate-intensity exercise. End with a five-minute cooldown at a slow pace, remembering to breathe deeply and savor the workout. Finish off with five minutes of stretching (the benefits of which you'll find in the next chapter).

To reduce fatigue, it can be helpful to work out to music, particularly music with a positive message and strong beat (Karageorghis et al., 2009). And if you really don't like exercise, sometimes any distraction can make it more enjoyable. Feel free to listen to a podcast or watch TV—doesn't matter if it's Anderson Cooper or *The Real Housewives*, as long as you're moving.

List some songs or podcasts you could work out to, and make a playlist:

_____   _____

_____   _____

_____   _____

_____   _____

_____   _____

_____   _____

_____   _____

You can also try a more varied aerobic workout. Here's a sample workout to get you going that doesn't require any extra equipment:

- ten knee bends (squats)

- ten push-ups (or hold a push-up position for thirty seconds)

- twenty sit-ups

- ten walking lunges

- thirty jumping jacks

Try starting with a five-minute jog or brisk walk. Then go from one exercise to the next, resting just long enough to start to catch your breath. Go through the whole circuit three times. End with a five-minute cooldown jog and five minutes of stretching.

If that seems too overwhelming, then just divide everything by five (for example, a one-minute warm-up jog, two squats, two push-ups, and so on) three times each. If you can do that three times for the first week, you're off to a good start. Then, next week, increase it by a little.

Start Where You Are

In terms of physical activity, where are you at? Are you sitting at a desk all day or even finding it difficult to get out of bed? Maybe the only exercise you get is walking to your car. Do you go to the gym occasionally? Do you play soccer once a week?

Side note to the reader who gets lots of exercise: it is possible to get too much. If you're running for hours at a time or doing very intense workouts or exercising everyday, then you may be stressing out your body. If you're on that end of the spectrum, sometimes focusing on sufficient rest can be beneficial.

You might not like where you are in terms of exercise, but the good news is that the less exercise you are getting now, the more you stand to benefit from increasing it. Whether you like where you are or not, you're still in the same place, so acknowledge it and make a plan to do what you can. Each little bit is helpful and contributes to an upward spiral. Don't worry about the exercise that you can't do or might not be able to do. Again, the small amount of exercise you actually do is infinitely more beneficial to you than some grand plan that you don't follow through with.

If you're finding it difficult to get any exercise at all, that's fine. Don't even think about forty-five minutes of exercise three times a week. Start smaller.

Slow and Steady Wins the Race

While Aesop's tortoise won the race by going slow and steady, it can be even more helpful to remember that your life isn't a race. But slow and steady is still often the best path forward.

The hardest part of exercise is starting it. So make it as simple to start as possible. Remove the barriers. If the thought of running five miles seems overwhelming, then run one mile. Does running at all seem completely unfeasible? Then start by walking around the block.

Once when I was having a tough time, that was my strategy. Every day I went for a walk. At first it was just around the block. But sometimes I made it longer—two blocks, three blocks, or wherever my feet took me.

There's something so easy about going for a walk, because it requires so little. For other forms of exercise, you might have to change clothes or shoes or work up the energy to do it or go somewhere like a gym or a basketball court. But to walk, you just open up the front door and keep going.

Starting off easy is particularly important if you're out of shape, because it's really easy to over-exert yourself. That doesn't mean you can't push yourself; just don't push yourself too much. Exertion when you're really out of shape can cause more negative emotions, particularly during high-intensity workouts (Frazao et al., 2016). Go for brief walks or even briefer jogs. If that's all you can manage for a few weeks, that's fine.

You don't need to run a marathon to start seeing benefits; even ten minutes of moderate exercise can improve energy and mood. Bumping it up to twenty minutes provides even more benefits (Hansen, Stevens, & Coast, 2001). No need to jump into huge amounts of exercise right away. Exercise studies showing improvements in pain and psychological health start with just ten minutes a day for many weeks before upping the workload (Schachter, Busch, Peloso, & Sheppard, 2003). So it's okay to start slow.

Tips for Facilitating Exercise

Many people complain that they lack the willpower to exercise. That's fine. The key to consistent good habits is to set things up so that you don't need so much willpower to do the things that are good for you. Use some of the suggestions from chapter 2, like scheduling it on your calendar. Below are some suggestions for relying on other avenues, like the dopamine system, to help get you going.

Tie Your Shoes

Famed UCLA basketball coach John Wooden started every season by asking his players to tie their shoes. The point was to get them to focus on bringing mindful intention and excellence to even the smallest tasks. I'm going to ask you to do something similar but even easier. You don't even need shoes with laces. You can wear sandals or flip-flops. All you have to do is put on your shoes and walk out the front door. If that's all you can manage, then that's fine. The world is a lot more accessible from your front steps when you're looking down the street than it is from your bedroom when you're staring at the ceiling.

You don't have to run a marathon. You don't even have to run a mile. Again, walking out the door is key, because from your spot on the couch, running seems way less appealing than it does when you're already out on the open road, breathing in a deep sunset.

The next time you're trying to work up the energy to go for a run, remember that you don't need to make the decision all at once. Taking small steps to get ready and changing your surroundings are both subconsciously processed by the hippocampus and the striatum, which can make it easier to exercise. Start by putting on your shoes. Go outside. Start walking. Try jogging a few steps. Set a timer for a minute. See how you feel then. If the big picture seems daunting, focus on the small picture. Take one small step in the right direction, and worry about the next step later.

Train for Something

Once, while working out at the UCLA track, I saw a famous actress also doing a workout. When I finally worked up the courage to ask what she was training for, her response was "Just life."

While it might be nice to think that we'll have the motivation to get in shape for "just life," it's much more likely to happen if we actually have a concrete goal in mind. Specific plans help engage the dopamine reward system to get us going. So sign up for a 5K or a short triathlon or maybe even a marathon! Don't just think about it, but put it on your calendar, fill out the form, and pay your money. That helps to engage the dopamine system even more, helping you stay motivated.

And if you can get a friend involved or join a team, even better. That's the movement spiral, social spiral, and goal spiral all rolled into one (see chapters 6 and 7 for more on the latter two).

What's an exercise goal that you could not just commit to but also sign up for?

_____

_____

_____

_____

_____

_____

Do It With Other People

Don't try to reinvent the wheel. Lots of people want to work out for a variety of reasons, and they get together to do it. Exercising with other people takes advantage of the social spiral (chapter 6). So join a class!

One Swedish study showed that joining an exercise class was even better for depression than receiving a standard treatment like seeing a psychologist or counselor (Helgadóttir, Hallgren, Ekblom, & Forsell, 2016). In that study, several hundred people signed up for a "modern fitness centre." I imagine modern fitness centers in Sweden are pretty nice places, with a chic Scandinavian design, like an upscale Ikea with yoga mats.

Importantly, the researchers found that the type of class did not make a difference. Some people took a light yoga class; others took moderate or even high-intensity aerobics classes. The hour-long classes met three times a week. When compared to the control group who underwent standard psychological treatment, all the exercise groups did better. After three months, the depression symptoms in the exercise groups dropped 30 to 40 percent more than the control group's.

This study shows that the intensity of exercise does not particularly matter, on average. Do it regularly. Do it with other people.

Making It Happen

To make this happen, use this space to write down activities you plan to do and when you plan to do them. Some suggestions for activities are taking a class, working out at the gym, walking or going for a hike or a run with someone you know, or joining a pick-up game of basketball.

To find suitable activities, look in your local paper, or contact the local YMCA or your city's Parks and Recreation department. Walk into a gym or fitness studio to see what they offer. Check out a local cultural or senior center, or search online (e.g., "Ultimate Frisbee in my area").

Write down any contact information that you need to make plans to meet someone or attend a class. If you need to sign up, then write in the third column the time and date that you will sign up. If you need to contact someone about getting together, use the third column to write down when you will do that. After making contact or signing up, write in the fourth column when the activity will occur.

Activity	Contact Info	Sign-Up Time/Date	Activity Time/Date

It's also helpful to keep a calendar of regular activities that you sign up for (you can use the activity-scheduling calendar from chapter 2 or your own day planner or calendar). Since the striatum works in a stimulus-response type way, having an event on your calendar triggers the striatum to help you actually do it.

Make It a Game

Wear a Fitbit or exercise monitor and make a game of it. See if you can get ten thousand steps a day. Way out of reach? Start with two thousand. Too easy? Bump it up to fifteen thousand.

If you're on a treadmill, think of the distance as your high score. See if you can beat your score from last time. Quantifying your goal helps engage the dopamine system, and making it a game keeps it fun.

Run, Forrest Run

You may remember the scene from the 1994 classic *Forrest Gump* in which Forrest just starts running and doesn't stop. Exercise doesn't always have to be meticulously planned. To put some excitement into it and to release more dopamine, make it an adventure. Put on your shoes and go—with no particular workout goal or destination in mind. Just step out the door and go wherever your curiosity takes you. If you get tired, rest. If you get thirsty, drink. Your body was made for moving. Enjoy it.

Conclusion

Some benefits of exercise may be apparent right away, but most can take weeks to fully manifest. The key is to continue doing it, even if just a little. Consistency will keep you on track.

What's the minimum amount of exercise you could commit to for a week? One push-up a day? Walking for thirty seconds? Whatever you're doing now, taking one small step forward is better than nothing.

But even if you don't feel better right away, remember that you are still delivering positive effects to your brain. So start slow, be patient, and remind yourself of all the neurochemical changes that are working behind the scenes to create an upward spiral.

Hopefully at this point, you have gotten your blood pumping at least once, or you've adventured out into the world. Getting moving is certainly one of the best ways to start an upward spiral, but it's not the only way. If by this point you're not yet training for the Olympics, doing five hundred sit-ups a day, or running a marathon, don't worry. The rest of the book is full of tips that not only create their own upward spirals but also will help with exercise.

And the relationship between the brain and the body doesn't end with exercise. There are even subtler forces at work in the body, shaping your brain's activity and chemistry. And that's next.

Chapter 4

The Breath and Body Spiral

Your brain depends on your body, and what happens in your body affects your brain. Chapter 3 talked about the effects of exercise, but there are, in fact, many ways that physical movements can change your brain's activity and chemistry. The body and brain exist in a feedback loop, like a microphone and speaker, and what happens in one affects the other.

Whether or not you are paying attention, your brain is constantly paying attention to the subtle signals from your body and its physiology, including measurements of heart rate, breathing, and muscle tension. By making small changes to your physiology, you change the signals going to the brain, and thus can have a big impact on anxiety and depression. This chapter explains how it's possible to change those signals through breathing, stretching, facial expressions, posture, and more, which can lead to dramatic improvements in mood and stress. But first, we'll explore a key aspect of your physiology that you might not be aware of.

The Rhythm of Your Heart

Your heart beats your whole life, but even when you're just sitting there, it does not beat steadily to the same rhythm. It speeds up and slows down like an expressive symphony conductor. This is called *heart rate variability*. In depression, the heart tends to beat more regularly, like a metronome. So people with depression have reduced heart rate variability (Blood et al., 2015). This is often a sign of too much stress—a chronic activation of the sympathetic nervous system's fight-or-flight response.

By contrast, high heart rate variability signifies activation of the body's *rest-and-digest mode* (parasympathetic nervous system), which can be accomplished through several techniques in this book. For example, over time, physical exercise causes big increases in heart rate variability. Breathing exercises can do the same. And as heart rate variability improves, so does depression.

The Power of Your Breath

If I were a betting man, I'd bet that the whole time you've been reading this book, you've been breathing—in, then out, then in again—and even though this has literally been sustaining your life, you probably weren't even aware of it until you just started reading about it. I don't bring this up to point out that your brain's automatic life support is something to be grateful for—it is, but we'll get to that in chapter 10. I bring it up because subtle changes in how you're breathing can have profound effects on your brain's emotional circuitry. So breathing not only keeps you alive, but also can improve your mood.

Breathing is controlled by several different parts of the brain. Primarily, there's a region of your brain stem, deep at the base of your skull, that makes sure you keep breathing in and out, in and out, all the minutes of your life: while you sleep, while you're distracted, while you're talking, while you're doing everything. Breathing is an automatic process, like your heartbeat or digestion. But unlike most automatic processes in the body, it's also under conscious control.

If you wanted, you could take a deep breath. Go for it.

If you wanted, you could pause for a moment before exhaling. Try.

You could breath rapidly or even hold your breath. You can't do that with most automatic processes in your body. Can you make your heart speed up or slow down? Can you stop your digestion? But since breathing is under some voluntary control, it offers one of the most powerful and simplest forms of changing your physiology.

Breathing affects the brain by altering signals in a special nerve called the *vagus nerve*, which originates in the brain stem and sends information back and forth from your body's internal organs to your brain. By changing your patterns of breathing, you're changing the information being sent, which can affect numerous brain regions as well as areas of the body.

Breathe in Through Your Nose

The erectile dysfunction drug Viagra was originally developed to benefit a different organ: the heart. It targeted a chemical-signaling pathway in the body that utilizes the gas nitric oxide, which relaxes blood vessels and lowers blood pressure. While nitric oxide signaling has heart-healthy benefits, scientists noticed in research trials that it also happens to help men get erections. Pfizer decided there was more money in that. But you can put this pathway to good use for its original intended purpose.

When you breathe in through your nose, you actually produce more nitric oxide than when you breathe in through your mouth (Törnberg et al., 2002).

So breathe in deeply through your nose, allowing nitric oxide to lower your blood pressure, and feel yourself relax.

How did it feel? Jot down what you experienced.

_____

_____

_____

_____

_____

Smooth and Slow

We'll start with slow and steady breathing, which helps push the brain away from fight-or-flight mode (sympathetic activity) to rest-and-digest mode (parasympathetic). This type of breathing has been shown to reduce anxiety (Chen, Huang, Chien, & Cheng, 2017) and the stress hormone cortisol as well as to diminish negative emotions (Ma et al., 2017).

To be most effective, it's helpful to pause briefly (one to four seconds) between the exhale and the inhale. Pausing allows you to make each breath intentional rather than habitual, and to appreciate it rather than take it for granted. This small pause has the effect of reducing sensations of pain and promoting increased heart rate variability (Russell, Scott, Boggero, & Carlson, 2017).

Are you ready?

Practice Slow, Steady Breathing

1. First, sit up or stand up straight, or lie down flat. We'll cover posture more in depth in a moment, but slouching constricts your ability to breathe deeply.

2. Let your breath out.

3. Now stop for a moment—breathing, that is. Not a long time. Just hold on a second or two so that your next breath isn't automatic.

4. Breathe in through your nose (assuming you don't have a cold). Make it intentional.

5. At the top of your inhale, pause for a second, just long enough to savor the air and to make the exhale intentional.

6. You can breathe out through your nose or mouth. Do what feels comfortable.

7. Pause again at the end of the exhale, and take another breath.

8. Utilize your diaphragm, the muscle above your belly and below your chest that is most effective at bringing air into your lungs. It's also possible to breathe using your chest muscles, but the effects are not as relaxing. When you breathe with your diaphragm, your belly expands but your chest does not move much. When breathing deeply, it's common to raise or tense your shoulders. Notice if you're doing it, and just relax them.

9. Now slow it down and smooth it out. As you inhale, count slowly up to five. Pause at the top, then exhale for the same slow count. This works out to about four to five breaths per minute. Breathing at that speed has been shown to soothe your brain from fight-or-flight mode to rest-and-digest.

10. Pay attention to the sensations coming from your body as you breathe. Feel your body expand on the inhale, and feel your muscles relax on the exhale.

Intentional breathing as a daily practice is a powerful way to reduce stress and start an upward spiral. The formal exercise is simple. Use the steps in the previous exercise to focus fully on your breathing. As you get used to the rhythm, it is no longer necessary to count to five for each breath, but it is always fine to count, particularly to re-center yourself.

To start, set a timer for three minutes, and just breathe while paying full attention to your breathing: the sounds, the actions, the physical sensations. If three minutes seems too daunting, then start with thirty seconds (just three breaths) on day one, a minute on day two, and so on, up to three minutes.

To stay on track, it helps to keep a breathing log for a week. After doing intentional breathing, use it to record the duration of the exercise and to rate on a 10-point scale how you feel afterward.

Breathing Log

	Duration	How do you feel after? (Use a scale of 1 to 10, in which 1=terrible and 10=amazing!)
Day 1		
Day 2		
Day 3		
Day 4		
Day 5		
Day 6		
Day 7		

Get Your Energy Up

Feeling low and slow? Sometimes your body needs a trick to get it going. You can do it by pushing your brain into active (sympathetic) mode instead of resting (parasympathetic). Tense your muscles. Stand up. Bounce around. Skip. Throw your hands in the air like you just don't care. Take five quick, forceful breaths. This is mimicking the physiological stress response, sending signals to the brain to start the cascade of energy release. Do you feel more energized?

_____

_____

_____

_____

_____

_____

Breathing During Stressful Moments

Practicing deep slow breathing regularly helps create a habit in your striatum that you can rely on in stressful situations. If you feel yourself getting stressed out, anxious, or overwhelmed, take a few breaths just like you've been practicing.

However, often when you're feeling panicked or stressed, it's very hard to control your breathing. And sometimes trying to control it just makes you more stressed out. So don't try to control it too much, but just make some tiny adjustments.

If you're feeling anxious or stressed, focus on lengthening the exhale. It can be helpful to make a sound like "shhhh." Or you can purse your lips as if blowing out a candle. This forces you to slow down your breathing rate. Or utilize a type of yogic breathing call *ujjayi*: to do this, exhale through your nose while constricting the back of your throat (almost like a hum, but without the vibration, just a smooth sound like waves rolling up the beach). Try this during your breathing practice. By making a sound, you are literally slowing down the air, and that will help elongate the exhale.

Here is an additional tip for changing your body's physiology during moments of stress: splash some cold water on your face. This triggers a reflex of the vagus nerve to slow down the heart.

Shaping Your Mood by Shaping Your Posture

How you stand or sit can impact your brain activity, affecting your mood, energy and confidence. People with depression tend to have a slumped or withdrawn posture, and improving posture leads to improvements in mood and energy levels (Wilkes, Kydd, Sagar, & Broadbent, 2017). While some studies of so-called power poses have been shown to be misleading or overblown, more prudent research has revealed that posture can have subtle effects on your mood and mind-set. These subtle effects are actually a great way to take advantage of the upward spiral, because they offer an opportunity to make small changes in the right direction.

Your posture affects your emotional experience of the world. For example, in one study, when people suffering from depression sat in slouched postures, their brains had a stronger bias toward negative information than when they sat up straight (Michalak, Mischnat, & Teismann, 2014). Other studies show that slouching makes the brain have to work harder to remember happy events (Tsai, Peper, & Lin, 2016). Sitting up straight eliminated the negative bias.

As with your facial expression, changing your posture won't change your mood dramatically, but it can enhance the mood that you're in—either positively or negatively. For example, if you're feeling down, having a slumped and withdrawn posture can worsen your mood. On the other hand, if you're feeling good or have done something good, then standing in an assertive or proud manner can enhance the effect—making subtle changes to your levels of testosterone (Smith & Apicella, 2017), and even increasing your enjoyment of activities (Peña & Chen, 2017).

You don't need to have great posture—just try diminishing your bad posture. Listen to your mother and stop slouching. If you're stuck lying in bed or on the couch, just standing up changes the electrical dynamics in your brain (Thibault, Lifshitz, Jones, & Raz, 2014). Use these simple changes to set yourself on the path to feeling better.

Practicing Good Sitting Posture

If you work at a desk job, you're probably stuck in a chair most of the day, so it's a great opportunity to practice good posture. At the top of every hour check in with your posture, and follow these steps:

1. Move your butt to the front of the chair, and place your feet flat on the floor.

2. Sit up straight.

3. On an inhale, shrug your shoulders up, and then on an exhale, relax them back and down. Let your shoulder blades tug slightly together as your chest opens. Notice if your head is jutting out in front of you; bring it back, so it rests directly above your spine.

4. At this point, you've probably stopped breathing and are tensing everything to keep it in place. Take another breath and relax. Try to let the posture happen rather than forcing it.

How does it feel to sit differently? Do you feel more focused or energized?

_____

_____

Mirror of the Mind

As St. Jerome once wrote, "The face is the mirror of the mind." But little did he know, it's actually a two-way mirror. Not only does your mood affect your facial expressions, but your facial expressions affect your mood. Simply by flexing or relaxing certain muscles in your face, you can actually start to change the way you feel.

While you can't smile away your negative feelings, your facial expressions can enhance or diminish the intensity of emotions that you're already feeling (Coles, Larsen, & Lench, 2017). So in moments where you feel a little happier, allow yourself to smile to amplify the emotion. If you feel appreciative of others, give them a smile: your friend, the supermarket cashier, a random person on the street. And if you're by yourself and feeling good, allow yourself to smile just for your own benefit. But don't feel you need to pretend like you're happy; that can have the reverse affect.

If you're feeling down or irritable, negative facial expressions enhance those emotions too. So, for negative emotions there's another solution.

Relax Your Face

In Camus's *The Stranger*, the main character becomes inexplicably filled with rage on the beach one day while squinting in the bright sun. He keeps harping on it, and it never made sense to me, but now neuroscience has an answer. One study found that having to squint in bright sunlight increased feelings of anger and hostility. These feelings were mitigated by facing away from the sun or by wearing sunglasses (Marzoli, Custodero, Pagliara, & Tommasi, 2013).

Maybe anger and hostility aren't your biggest issues, but wearing sunglasses or finding some shade can be a simple small step—one of many pushing your neural circuits in the right direction.

In general, when your facial muscles are tense, it's easy to feel emotionally tense. Are you tensing your eyebrows or frown muscles, or are you clenching your jaw? You don't need to turn that frown upside down, but at least stop flexing those muscles. Take a deep breath and let go of the tension in your face.

Relax Your Muscles to Relax Your Mind

The muscles in your face aren't the only ones that affect your mood. Tight muscles in your body also have a negative effect on mood and depression. For one, they increase physical pain and discomfort. Tight muscles can make exercise more difficult, and sometimes just sitting there, you can feel uncomfortable in your own body. Secondly, tight muscles increase stress and anxiety. Tense muscles send a signal to your brain that you're tense and stressed. It also works the other way: stress can increase muscle tension. Sometimes mental relaxation helps relax the muscles, but since stress depends on a feedback loop, it's often easier to start with physical relaxation.

Stretching

Stretching can help improve mood. It also releases pain-relieving endorphins. If you're finding it difficult to start an exercise program from the previous chapter, perhaps start with a stretching program.

When you're stretching, it's important to not stretch to the point of pain. If anything you're doing is painful, then you're doing it too hard. That doesn't mean it won't be uncomfortable at times. It will almost certainly be uncomfortable, because your muscles are tight. As you stretch your muscles, focus on breathing and relaxing. Notice if the sensations are painful or just uncomfortable—a component of mindfulness from chapter 8. Relax into the stretch. If it's so uncomfortable that you can't relax, then ease off a bit.

Progressive Muscle Relaxation

While a lot of neuroscience research is fairly new, scientists have been studying the effects of relaxation for over a hundred years. In 1925, an American researcher named Edmond Jacobson pioneered a technique called *progressive muscle relaxation* (PMR).

Ever feel like you have tight muscles? Interestingly, your muscles don't tighten on their own. Your muscles are only tight because your brain is sending a signal to them that they should flex.

But since your brain does lots of things that you're not consciously aware of, you probably don't realize when it's happening.

So how can you stop unintentionally flexing your muscles? Well you can start by flexing them intentionally and then relaxing them. This is one of the key aspects of PMR.

Practicing relaxation can help improve anxiety and depression overall (Fung & White, 2012). It can also help during difficult situations, such as recovering from surgery (Essa, Ismail, & Hassan, 2017). It affects both the body and the brain—reducing activity in the insula and anterior cingulate—regions that contribute to the experience of pain and physical discomfort (Kobayashi & Koitabashi, 2016). With continued practice, the results can last for months into the future.

Practicing Progressive Muscle Relaxation

Find a quiet couch to lie down on, or perhaps a yoga mat. Take a few deep breaths to start, letting go of anything that is bothering you. Set aside your worries for a moment—and maybe they'll forget to come back.

PMR involves tensing muscles and relaxing them as you work your way around your body. Remember that there's nothing you need to do to try to relax. After tensing a muscle, just stop tensing. No need to try hard to do anything else.

As you tense a muscle, breathe in. Hold your breath and the tension for a moment, and then let go of the breath and the tension in the muscle. Now that you've got the basic idea, here we go.

Start with the muscles of your face, including your jaw. Clench them tight as you inhale. Hold for a moment. Then relax. Repeat this two more times.

Tense your shoulders and neck.

After that, move on to clenching your fists and tensing your arms.

Tense and relax your abdomen and torso.

Tense and relax your buttocks.

Tense and relax your feet and legs.

When you've finished, lie there for a few moments breathing naturally. Enjoy the sensation of having wrung out the tension from your body like a sponge.

To facilitate relaxation, you can also visualize relaxing imagery. Imagining your limbs relaxing actually reduces the reactivity of the neurons that control your muscles—calming your body from the brain down (Kato & Kanosue, 2018). You can also visualize yourself in a relaxing place—immersing yourself in the feelings, sounds, sights, and smells of a peaceful world. This type of imagery can even lower your blood pressure (Crowther, 1983).

Try adding visualization to stretching or progressive muscle relaxation. Imagine the feeling of your muscles letting go. Picture yourself on a warm beach, listening to the waves crash nearby, or in a cabin in the woods, wrapped in a cozy blanket with the fire crackling nearby and rain pattering on the roof.

Yoga and Modern Neuroscience

Yoga combines strengthening, stretching, breathing and mindfulness, so it could equally have been introduced in the chapters on exercise or mindfulness. One of yoga's strengths is that it can create an upward spiral in so many ways.

Across numerous scientific studies, yoga has been shown to be helpful for depression and anxiety (Cramer, Lauche, Langhorst, & Dobos, 2013). It has a wide array of effects on the brain. For example, yoga's anti-anxiety effect results from the fact that it targets the same calming neurotransmitter system (GABA) that anti-anxiety medications like Valium and Xanax target (Streeter, Gerbarg, Saper, Ciarulo, & Brown, 2012). Frequent yoga has been shown to enhance the size of the hippocampus, a sign of a healthy brain (Villemure, Čeko, Cotton, & Bushnell, 2015). It also can improve pain tolerance by enhancing the size of the brain region responsible for internal sensations (the insula) (Villemure, Čeko, Cotton, & Bushnell, 2014).

Yoga Poses

While practitioners of yoga have touted its mental benefits for decades, if not centuries, modern science has been slow to catch up. But now yoga has been studied in rigorous scientific fashion. One study showed that certain poses have the biggest boost on mood: back bends and chest opening poses (Shapiro & Cline, 2004). And indeed, adding yoga to more traditional treatments of depression provides significant benefits (de Manincor et al., 2016).

A Quick Chest Opener

For a quick way to take advantage of the mood-boosting effects of opening your chest, try this simple maneuver. It can be done sitting or standing.

Raise your chin and look up.

Open your arms out wide slowly, with palms facing up as if you're embracing the sky.

Take a deep breath and let it out.

While yoga has longer-term effects, it can also be a great quick way to boost your mood. Even a single session of yoga can have an immediate effect in reducing the fight-or-flight response, improving immune system function, lowering stress hormones and actually elevating testosterone, which increases vitality (Eda et al., 2018).

One of the easiest ways to learn yoga is to sign up for a beginner-friendly yoga class. The type of yoga doesn't matter as much as simply doing it. Going to a yoga class is likely more powerful than practicing on your own because it incorporates so many more aspects of an upward spiral (like being around people, and changing your environment), but practicing on your own is still beneficial. Below are some postures you can try, and there are many YouTube videos you could follow along with.

Yoga Poses and Movements

A full yoga practice may take an hour or more, but doing a shorter practice can still be beneficial. Doing it regularly really helps. For example, I do about two minutes of yoga each morning, and it really helps me be focused, calm, and productive.

As you move into each pose, hold the pose for a breath or two. Practice the same slow, smooth breathing as you practiced earlier in this chapter—it's a key aspect of yoga that helps in reducing depressive symptoms. Make each breath intentional, with a slight pause in between, perhaps even trying the ujjayi breath.

Cobra

Start lying face down, with the tops of your feet also facing down. Place your palms next to your chest as if you're about to do a push-up, but tucked in close. Keep your elbows close to your sides, and squeeze your shoulder blades together. Push up and arch your back slightly so that your chin lifts and you are looking several feet in front of you. Breathe for a couple breaths and slowly lower yourself back down.

Cat/Cow Movement

Get on your hands and knees, with your shoulders above your hands and your hips above your knees. As you exhale, tuck your chin into your chest and round your back. As you inhale, lift up your chin and look up as you arch your back. Repeat slowly five times.

Mountain Pose With Raised Arms

Stand up straight, with your arms at your sides. Take a deep breath in as you raise your arms in front of you, palms facing each other—continuing until your arms are reaching toward the sky. Raise your chin and look up slightly as you do so. Relax your shoulders.

How do you feel after doing this sequence of yoga poses? Jot down anything that you notice.

_____

_____

_____

_____

_____

_____

Music for the Soul

They say that music tames the savage beast, but it can also tame the savage limbic system. Relaxing music reduces the stress hormone cortisol and increases oxytocin, which is the same chemical that helps us feel connected to other people (Nilsson, 2009). During stressful situations, relaxing music lowers your heart rate and blood pressure (Knight & Rickard, 2001). Unsurprisingly, these stress-reducing aspects of music are beneficial in dealing with depression.

But music can also be exciting, and stimulating, and that's just as important in depression. As a song builds, it can actually increase your heart rate and blood pressure (Bernardi et al., 2009). Music releases endorphins and increases activity in the nucleus accumbens, which help to reduce pain and give you tingles of joy down your spine (Blood & Zatorre, 2001). It can decrease anxiety and increase heart rate variability (Nakahara, Furuya, Obata, Masuko, & Kinoshita, 2009).

Here are some ways to include more music in your life:

☐ Play an instrument you love or take lessons on one that you've always wanted to learn how to play.

☐ Sing in the shower.

☐ Sing in the car.

☐ Tap along to the radio.

☐ Join a band.

☐ Sing at church.

☐ Go to a concert or to a sing-along.

☐ Play more music around the house while you cook, clean, and hang out (buying a nice speaker will facilitate that).

Bring more music into your life that helps you feel good. Make a playlist of songs that that can help calm you down and another playlist of songs that can help you feel more excitement and energy. You can use this space to create a list.

Calming Songs	Exciting Songs

Raise Your Body Temperature

Humans are warm-blooded animals, which means we can regulate our own body temperatures, but that doesn't mean we do it in an ideal way. It turns out that increasing your body temperature slightly can improve depressive symptoms for several days (Janssen et al., 2016). Increasing body temperature stimulates the region of the brain stem that produces serotonin, which can have widespread effects throughout the brain.

Here are some ways to raise your body temperature:

☐ Go in a sauna.

☐ Take a hot bath or shower.

☐ Exercise.

☐ Drink something warm like coffee, tea, or hot chocolate.

☐ Sit by the fire.

☐ Put on warmer clothes.

☐ Wrap yourself in a blanket.

Conclusion

You don't have total control over your body's physiology, but you do have some control, and that's often enough to create an upward spiral. Recognize how your body affects your feelings, both positively and negatively. Take care of your body, and it will take care of your brain.

Chapter 5

The Sleep Spiral

The writer Ernest Hemingway once said, "I love sleep. My life has a tendency to fall apart when I'm awake, you know?" Perhaps you can relate. But sleep isn't just an opportunity to escape consciousness for a while; it provides a means of replenishing the brain, restoring energy, improving mood, and reducing both stress and pain.

Sleep disturbances—either insomnia or sleeping too much—are a common symptom of depression. Difficulties with sleep are an unfortunate downward spiral, because poor sleep quality tends to create poor sleep habits—and even poorer sleep quality—impacting mood and anxiety along the way. In fact, if poor sleep isn't addressed on its own, it increases the risk of developing depression in the first place (Sivertsen et al., 2012).

Given that we spend about one-third of our lives asleep, and because sleep impacts so many of the neural circuits of depression, improving the quality of your sleep is a great way to start, or enhance, an upward spiral. This chapter focuses on the effects of good (and bad) sleep on the brain, and will lead you through simple tips to improve your sleep.

Sleep and the Brain

Before jumping into specific recommendations, I'd like to first explain the neuroscience of sleep. I'll then focus on sleep's effects on the brain and depression so that you can see all of the benefits of the sleep spiral.

Sleep Architecture

Sleep isn't just a time for your brain to turn off. There's actually a lot happening, even though you're not aware of it. Approximately every ninety minutes, your brain cycles through various stages of sleep (stages 1 to 4 and then REM sleep). The relative time spent in each stage shifts throughout the night as your brain maintains a delicate balance. This is known as *sleep architecture*.

Waking up in the middle of the night disrupts your sleep architecture. In fact, the biggest benefit from sleep comes not from the total amount of time you sleep but from the amount of continuous sleep that you get. Six straight hours of sleep is more restorative than eight hours of sleep with disruptions.

The Brain's Internal Clock

While your brain activity during sleep is important, it's just part of the story. There are actually key neural systems at work around the clock; specifically, this is your brain's internal biological clock. Your brain's clock is important in both quality sleep and daytime alertness, and it controls hormonal fluctuations throughout the day. The brain's clock has many functions and is referred to as your *circadian rhythms*.

Your circadian rhythms release the stress hormone cortisol in the morning to prepare you to face the day (that's a good thing) and melatonin at night to prepare your brain for sleep. Circadian rhythms are primarily controlled by the hypothalamus, so they're intimately connected with the limbic system and your emotions. Later, this chapter will cover how to make the most of your circadian rhythms to get high-quality sleep.

Brain Benefits of Sleep

Below are some of the brain benefits that come from making the most of your circadian rhythms and high quality sleep. Check off any effects that are particularly important to you.

☐ Good sleep elevates mood.

As you might imagine, improving sleep quality can improve mood. For one, insomnia can disrupt prefrontal functioning, and the prefrontal cortex is important in regulating the emotional limbic system. Fortunately, making use of the suggestions in this chapter can restore proper prefrontal functioning (Altena et al., 2008). Sleep is also important in proper communication between the prefrontal cortex and the limbic system (Wierzynski, Lubenov, Gu, & Siapas, 2009). Lastly, quality sleep is important in regulating the serotonin system, as consistent bad sleep actually reduces sensitivity of serotonin receptors (Meerlo, Havekes, & Steiger, 2015).

☐ Good sleep reduces stress.

Improving sleep reduces stress hormones (Lopresti, Hood, & Drummond, 2013). It also increases prefrontal norepinephrine signaling, which is important in appropriately responding to stress (Kim, Chen, McCarley, & Strecker, 2013).

☐ Good sleep supports healthy habits.

Quality sleep affects the brain's reward circuitry. Disrupting sleep biases the brain toward responding to short-term rewards instead of long-term ones. For example, getting sufficient sleep reduces the brain's differential response to unhealthy foods in the orbitofrontal cortex and insula (St-Onge, Wolfe, Sy, Shechter, & Hirsch, 2014). Thus, quality sleep makes it easier to make healthy choices that are good for the long term.

☐ Good sleep decreases pain and discomfort.

Quality sleep enhances release of pain-relieving endorphins (Campbell et al., 2013). So it can be a great way to reduce pain and discomfort. Unfortunately, pain can disrupt sleep, which is one of the reasons that chronic pain is so insidious. But while you often can't control your pain directly, taking other recommendations in this chapter and the rest of this book will help through indirect pathways.

☐ Good sleep improves clear thinking.

Improving sleep improves clear thinking for several reasons. First, quality sleep improves function of the prefrontal cortex (Altena et al. 2008). Second, sleep is essential for removing metabolic breakdown products from the brain that accumulate as a result of the brain's chemical reactions throughout the day (Xie et al., 2013). If this chemical junk isn't removed, it can interfere with neural processing.

Why are these benefits of sleep important to you?

_____

_____

_____

_____

The recommendations in this chapter will help you achieve them.

Getting in the Way of Good Sleep

Your bedtime routine, as well as what you do throughout the day, can impact the quality of your sleep. The daily practices and habits that can affect sleep quality and daytime alertness all fall under one broad term: *sleep hygiene*.

   Just as good dental hygiene keeps your teeth strong and bright, good sleep hygiene improves the quality of your sleep and boosts your daytime energy and alertness. But before I describe what constitutes good sleep hygiene, let's focus on becoming aware of what you're currently doing.

Examining Your Sleep Hygiene

What is your current bedtime routine, or what do you do during the hour before trying to go to sleep?

_____

_____

_____

_____

_____

_____

Do you do any of the following? Check off anything that you do at least a couple times a week.

☐ Use phone, tablet, or laptop in bed

☐ Go to sleep really late

☐ Go to sleep at different times

☐ Wake up at different times

☐ Stay out late on the weekends

☐ Work the night shift

☐ Get disturbed while you're trying to sleep

☐ Not get any exercise during the day

☐ Not get much sunlight during the day

☐ Consume a lot of coffee, tea, soda, chocolate, or other caffeinated foods or drinks

☐ Drink alcohol at night

☐ Consume caffeine after 4:00 p.m.

☐ Smoke

☐ Sleep in a noisy environment

☐ Sleep in a room with lots of lights (from the window or from electronic devices)

☐ Do stressful activities (like work) right before bed or in bed

☐ Do physical activity (like exercise) less than two hours before bed

If you consistently do any of the items on this list, then your sleep quality may be affected. Poor sleep quality may be making your depression worse, so improving your sleep hygiene is a great place to start.

Practicing Good Sleep Hygiene

Below is a description of good sleep hygiene practices. Check off any practices that are already part of your daily routine. Circle any practice that isn't currently part of your routine.

☐ **Have a regular bedtime.**

Based on your circadian rhythms, your brain releases the neurotransmitter melatonin to prepare for sleep. Unfortunately, you can't just tell your brain when your bedtime is; it has to be trained by going to bed at the same time every night. It's fine to vary a little, and to occasionally stay up late, but there should be a clear time you think of as your bedtime. You'll fall asleep easier, and the sleep you get will be of higher quality.

☐ **Get some sun during the day.**

Your circadian rhythms get reset every morning by bright light, so if you're in a dimly lit office all day, your internal clock can drift out of synch. Take a few minutes in the morning to go walking in the sunshine. And throughout the day, keep the light up bright, sit near a window, or take breaks to walk outside. These steps will enhance release of melatonin at night.

☐ **Dim the lights at night.**

Bright lights at night disrupt melatonin. You don't need to walk around in the dark, but turn off unnecessary lights or use the dimmer, particularly as bedtime approaches. Blue light is the bigger culprit, so use the nighttime mode available on many phones and tablets. And when you turn off the lights, even little LED lights on electronic devices can be very bright, so cover them up.

☐ **Sleep for just long enough to feel refreshed the next day.**

In general, the older you get, the less sleep you need—about eight and a half hours in college and about an hour less by age sixty. But that's just the average person—you might need a little more or a little less than that. While you may be concerned that you don't have enough time for sleep, the good news is that quality is more important than quantity. And getting more than you need is not actually better for you. In fact, it's actually healthier to get slightly too little sleep than too much (Strand et al., 2016). You can't save sleep up, so don't try to get extra for later; it'll just mess up your sleep the following night.

☐ **Make your bedroom comfortable.**

Sleep requires a calming of the sympathetic nervous system, which is harder if you're uncomfortable. Make your bedroom a calming environment; remove or hide things that excite you or stress you out (like a TV or computer). Pretend you're designing a spa. That might sound silly, but the hippocampus and striatum are both impacted by environmental cues that indicate a calming environment, triggering associations with sleep and relaxation. If your room is too hot or too bright or too noisy, then do something about it. Try a white noise machine for soothing sounds. If there's something about your bedroom you can't change, then the only positive path forward is acceptance, which will be covered in chapter 8.

☐ **Your bedroom is for sleep and sex.**

Don't do work or your taxes or any activities that are stressful or take a lot of focus and thinking. Restful, calming activities like reading are okay (unless your insomnia is really bad, in which case, read somewhere else). That way, your brain associates your bed with sleep, and it will induce sleepiness.

☐ **Don't take naps.**

Taking a nap will make it more difficult to fall asleep at bedtime. To be clear, taking a brief nap can help you feel better after your nap, but it will not help you fall asleep better that night, and it won't help you feel better the next day. An occasional nap is okay, but don't make napping a regular part of your routine.

☐ **Create a calming routine to prepare your brain for sleep.**

Having a bedtime ritual helps you separate yourself from the hectic nature of the rest of your day. It prepares your brain for sleep. If you're running around, putting out fires all day, and then just plop into bed, your brain still needs to wind down, and you may have difficulty falling asleep. A bedtime ritual might be to brush your teeth, wash your face, go to the bathroom, and then read for a few minutes. Or maybe you include herbal tea as part of that, or reading to your kids beforehand, or writing in a gratitude journal—these should be pleasant, nonstressful activities.

☐ **Avoid caffeine, alcohol, and nicotine.**

Both caffeine and nicotine are stimulants that may make it harder to fall asleep. And even if you're able to fall asleep, stimulants can disrupt your sleep architecture and make sleep lest restful. Some people are more sensitive to caffeine than others, so even late afternoon caffeine may be a problem. Lastly, alcohol may make it easier to fall asleep, but it's likely to make you wake up sooner, and when used habitually, it disrupts sleep architecture (Roehrs, Hyde, Blaisdell, Greenwald, & Roth, 2006). While it's understandable that you might want to use these substances, as they often provide short-term benefits, they unfortunately have long-term negative consequences. Utilizing many of the suggestions in this book may help reduce your reliance on them.

☐ **Be conscientious of eating and drinking.**

Don't eat a big meal right before bed, as indigestion can interfere with sleep. On the other hand, if you find that you're distracted by hunger, it's okay to have a light snack. The same goes for liquids. Don't drink too much in the evening, as needing to pee can disrupt your sleep architecture.

☐ **Exercise.**

Make physical activity a regular part of your life (see chapter 3). Exercise has a synchronizing effect on your circadian rhythms and reduces stress, leading to improved sleep. Exercising late at night delays melatonin release and can make it harder to fall asleep, but early evening exercise has the most beneficial effect.

Getting Ready for Quality Sleep

Describe how your current sleep hygiene practices may be getting in the way of quality sleep and daytime alertness.

_____

_____

_____

_____

What habits could you implement right away? Do you foresee any challenges to putting these better sleep hygiene habits into practice?

_____

_____

_____

Can you see how you might implement better sleep hygiene despite these potential challenges?

_____

_____

_____

Journaling and the Power of Writing

Language has a powerful effect on the human brain. As a result, there are many ways that the simple act of writing can improve the quality of sleep and other symptoms of depression.

Expressive Writing

Expressive writing focuses on exploring your deepest thoughts and feelings about a trauma, anxiety, or other negative event. And even though this chapter is about sleep, this kind of writing has many beneficial effects beyond improved sleep. It helps attach language to your deepest emotions, allowing the prefrontal cortex to more strongly regulate the amygdala (Memarian, Torre, Halton, Stanton, & Lieberman, 2017). This not only integrates your thoughts and feelings but also can reduce the intensity of negative feelings.

Write About a Difficult Event

Write about a difficult event from your past or any other event that keeps running through your mind and bringing up negative thoughts and feelings. Set a timer for fifteen minutes, and write about your deepest thoughts and feelings about the event. Don't shy away from the hard ones, as writing about those provides the most benefit. Don't worry about grammar, spelling, writing well, or even making sense—you just have to keep writing.

If you can't think of anything to write before time is up, just keep writing about how you can't think of anything to write until another thought pops into your head. If you can't get a handle on your feelings, then it's perfectly fine to write about how you can't quite describe what you're feeling. Just keep going. Some space is provided here. You can also write in your journal or use your computer.

_____

_____

_____

_____

_____

_____

_____

_____

_____

_____

_____

_____

_____

_____

_____

_____

_____

_____

_____

_____

_____

_____

_____

_____

_____

You don't have to share this writing with anyone, and you don't even have to read it. It's easy to ignore unpleasant thoughts and feelings, but the key is to use this as an opportunity to explore what's floating around in there.

Repeat this process for three days in a row. If the same event is still weighing on your mind, keep writing about the same event, but try to integrate your thoughts and insights from your previous writings.

Writing Down Your Worries

Worrying activates the prefrontal cortex and often gets the limbic system and the stress response involved, all making it more difficult to fall asleep. Sometimes your worries are irrational or exaggerated (more on that topic later in the chapter), but your worries can also be totally rational, such as when you're thinking about all the things you need to do tomorrow. One study showed that people who wrote to-do lists fell asleep faster (Scullin, Krueger, Ballard, Pruett, & Bliwise, 2018). That's where this next simple writing exercise can come in handy.

Make a To-Do List

As part of your bedtime routine, spend a few minutes writing down a to-do list of all the things that you're worrying about. Now you can rest assured that you will remember to do these things tomorrow.

_____   _____

_____   _____

_____   _____

_____   _____

_____   _____

You may want to keep a pad and pen next to your bed. If you think of anything that you don't want to forget, you can just jot it down as a reminder to think about it tomorrow.

Expressing Gratitude

Taking a brief moment to write down things you're grateful for can actually improve the quality of your sleep. As you're preparing to go to sleep, think back over the past day and write down three to five things, big or small, that you're grateful for (such as a new job or a delicious lunch), or people in your life that you appreciate.

1. _____

2. _____

3. _____

4. _____

5. _____

Keep a Sleep Diary

To really get a handle on how bad your sleep is, it's helpful to keep a sleep diary. In fact, if you went to a sleep specialist, the first thing you'd be asked to do is to keep a sleep diary. A weekly sleep diary gives you a sense of where you're at, and you may even start to notice patterns that will allow you to start problem solving on your own. And if you end up going to a sleep specialist, bring your sleep diary to show them. (Visit http://www.newharbinger.com/42426 to download a printable version of this weekly sleep diary.)

Weekly Sleep Diary

Write in the day and date. In the morning, write down what time you went to bed, when you woke up, how you felt upon waking, how many hours you slept, and any nighttime wakefulness or disturbances. At night, write down if you exercised, consumed caffeine or alcohol, or took any medication that day, and, if so, how much and when. Describe your bedtime routine, or what you did in the hour before bed, such as shower, brush teeth, or watch TV.

Day/Date	Complete this part in the morning.		
	Bedtime	Waking Time	How You Feel
Day 1			
Day 2			
Day 3			
Day 4			
Day 5			
Day 6			
Day 7			

Hours Slept	Night-time Waking	Complete at night.	
		Exercise, Caffeine, Alcohol, Medications	Bedtime Routine

Cognitive Behavioral Therapy for Insomnia

Good sleep hygiene is good for anyone, but if you've got really bad insomnia, you may need to rely on more advanced techniques. Cognitive behavioral therapy for insomnia (CBT-I) can be extremely helpful in dealing with the sleep issues that arise from depression (Perlis, Jungquist, Smith, & Posner, 2006). Some of the strategies used by CBT-I are helpful all the time (such as many of the cognitive strategies), but some of the behavioral strategies are used only in the short term to get your sleep back on track.

The problem with insomnia is not just the lack of sleep but also the anxiety caused by the uncertainty and uncontrollability of sleep. So if things are really bad, the first goal is to simply improve your brain's ability to fall asleep.

Falling asleep is not something you can do just by trying. In fact, like quicksand, the harder you try and the more you struggle, the worse it gets. Sounds like a downward spiral to me. So we're going to make it easier to fall asleep without trying.

The techniques presented here are just the tip of the iceberg when it comes to CBT-I. Some you can implement easily on your own, but others may be a little tougher. Remember that you don't have to do everything by yourself. You can also consult other CBT-I resources, and a trained mental health professional can help guide you through them.

Setting a Fixed Rise Time

One common response to insomnia is to try to sleep in as late as possible. The thinking goes that when you can finally sleep, you might as well get as much as you can. It sounds reasonable, but the issue with overcoming insomnia isn't primarily about getting enough sleep; it's about relearning how to fall asleep and stay asleep. And, unfortunately, sleeping in can get in the way. Furthermore, if you suffer from the opposite of insomnia and find yourself sleeping all the time (that is, *hypersomnia*), setting an alarm is even more important.

One of the issues with sleeping in is that it disrupts your circadian rhythms. Sleeping in also makes it more likely that you won't be tired at bedtime. So if you're going to set a fixed time to go to bed, set a fixed time to rise as well.

Set an alarm for a reasonable time, and set the same alarm every day of the week. A consistent rise time is particularly helpful for improving sleep if you're unemployed or have a nontraditional job.

Use this space to write down the time you will set your alarm for. Then write down any complaints you have about needing to get up at the set time, so that it'll save you time having to run through them all when your alarm goes off.

_____

_____

_____

_____

When the alarm goes off, don't hit the snooze button. Just get up. There's no way to will yourself out of bed—you just have to do it. Much of recovery is simply making honest promises to yourself and then keeping them.

Restricting Time in Bed

How can you avoid difficulty falling asleep or staying asleep? By making yourself sleepier. How can you make yourself sleepier? Simple—by getting less sleep. It may seem counterintuitive to deprive yourself of sleep, but by doing it intentionally in a structured way, you can retrain your brain to fall asleep faster and to stay asleep. This is a difficult strategy, because you will likely feel worse for a few days or weeks, and it should only be used if you've got really bad insomnia. However, if you have bipolar disorder, sleep apnea, or a seizure disorder, this strategy should be avoided. This is actually a complex treatment and is best guided by an expert, but I'll provide you with a simplified form.

To implement this strategy, review your weekly sleep diary and figure out your average time asleep. Then multiply this number by 1.1, and that's your new goal for time in bed.

Let's say you normally try to go to sleep at 11:00 p.m. and wake up at 7:00 a.m., but you end up getting only 5.5 hours of sleep on average. Take 5.5 and multiply it by 1.1 (5.5 hours x 1.1 = 6.05 hours). We'll round that to six hours. To figure out your new bedtime, keep your rise time fixed, and then calculate backwards. So if your new target time in bed is six hours, then your new bedtime will be 1:00 a.m (that's 7:00 a.m. minus six hours). So instead of trying to go to sleep at 11:00 p.m., tossing and turning for hours or waking up in the middle of the night, you're now going to wait until 1:00 a.m. before crawling into bed. After four days, if you're falling asleep quickly and mostly staying asleep, then push your bedtime fifteen minutes earlier and repeat, readjusting every four days. Maintain a sleep diary to help you keep track of everything, and if your targeted time in bed is less than six hours, you should seek professional supervision.

You will definitely feel very tired, but after retraining your brain to fall asleep faster and stay asleep, you'll eventually work your way up to a full night of sleep.

Stimulus Control

The goal of stimulus control is to utilize the benefits of classical conditioning, which simply means using a cue to trigger a behavior. In this case, the cue is your bed, and the behavior is falling asleep.

Ideally, your climbing into bed should be followed quickly by sleep. And, in fact, entering your bedroom at night should be followed shortly by climbing into bed and then sleeping. Each step prepares the brain for the next step.

But now, entering your bedroom at night might be followed by anxiety and worry, and the same goes for climbing into bed. So to break that association, don't spend time in your bed, or even your bedroom, when you're not sleeping.

Wait until you're very sleepy, and then go into your bedroom and climb into bed. If you don't fall asleep within a reasonable amount of time, get up and leave your bedroom, and do something relaxing until you feel like you're about to fall asleep again. Repeat as needed until sleep comes more naturally.

Identifying Unhelpful Thoughts About Sleep

While you are getting ready for bed—or already under the sheets—unhelpful thoughts may pop into your head that threaten to disrupt a good night of sleep. These unhelpful thoughts can fall into different categories, including unrealistic expectations, selective attention, black-and-white thinking, catastrophizing, and *should-thoughts* about what you think you should be doing. Just as at other times, it can be helpful to identify and challenge these thoughts by reframing them with more realistic or helpful thinking.

Unrealistic Expectations

Unhelpful thoughts can be about comparing everything to an unnecessarily high, unhelpful, or impossible standard. Such unrealistic expectations can take the form of *I have to get eight hours of sleep every night or I'll fall apart.*

Reframing: The reality is that one night of bad sleep won't really have much of a negative effect. In fact, even if you feel like you've been lying awake for an hour, it's common to fall asleep briefly and then wake up and not even realize it. You might say to yourself, *One night of bad sleep won't kill me.* Or, *I may have already fallen asleep briefly without noticing it.* Or *Just lying here, I'm getting some rest.* Reframing will lower your anxiety and help you eventually fall asleep.

Selective Attention

Using selective attention is paying particular attention to the negative aspects of a situation, often distorting or exaggerating the truth of or the relevance of negative information. *I never sleep well* is an example of this kind of thinking.

Reframing: Whenever you catch yourself thinking *always* or *never*, you should question whether you're using selective attention. Look for counter-examples to your thoughts or other positive information. You can reframe your negative thinking to more accurately reflect reality: *Sometimes I don't sleep well.* This thought is less likely to cause anxiety or get in the way of sleeping.

Black-or-White Thinking

Black-or-white thinking means dividing everything into categories that are either good or bad; doing this can increase stress and decrease feelings of self-efficacy. An example at bedtime would be *If I get a good night's sleep, everything will go well, but if I get a bad night of sleep, everything will be terrible.*

Reframing: Like pretty much everything in life, your sleep does not fit neatly into the two categories of good or bad. There are gradations. *One bad night of sleep is unpleasant, but it won't really have a big impact on my life, and one good night of sleep won't solve all my problems.* There are usually some good and bad aspects in everything. Allow some space for nuance.

Catastrophizing

Catastrophizing means assuming that the worst-case scenario will happen: *If I can't sleep I won't be able to focus at work, and then I'll get fired.*

Reframing: Recognize that the worst-case scenario is unlikely, and that it's much more likely that things will turn out better. *Given the hundreds of sleepless nights I've already had worrying about the worst-case scenario, I can see that the worst case is pretty unlikely.*

Should-Thoughts

It is not helpful to focus on how things should or shouldn't be. An example would be *I did all the suggestions in this book. I should be asleep by now.*

Reframing: Any time you use the words "should," "shouldn't," or "have to," there's often a more nuanced and descriptive way of thinking about the situation. For example, *I want to get a good night of sleep* or *I am upset that I'm not asleep right now.*

Reframing Unhelpful Thoughts

What are some of your unhelpful thoughts that have increased your anxieties about sleep or contributed to your sleep problems? Have you been catastrophizing or using black-or-white thinking, or having any other kind of unhelpful thoughts? Are these thoughts true, partially true, or perhaps just plain wrong? Write down three examples of your own unhelpful thoughts. Try to name the thought category or categories that these thoughts fall into, but don't sweat it if you can't. Then challenge each thought by reframing it with more helpful thinking.

Unhelpful thought: _____

_____

Reframing: _____

_____

_____

Unhelpful thought: _____

_____

Reframing: _____

_____

_____

Unhelpful thought: _____

_____

Reframing: _____

_____

_____

Conclusion

The recommendations in this chapter should greatly improve the quality of your sleep, but that doesn't mean every night will be blissful. Even if there are some nights you can't sleep, as long as you keep doing your best to follow this workbook, then you're on the right track. If you can't accept the occasional night of bad sleep, then you're setting yourself up for a downward spiral.

Lack of acceptance often makes things worse, because when you're lying there trying to fall asleep, repeating over and over in your head how terrible it is that you can't sleep, you're only succeeding in stressing yourself out. And maybe you're even criticizing yourself for how you're making things worse. Downward spirals are so insidious.

We'll cover acceptance more in chapter 8. Acceptance is a powerful way to create an upward spiral and often the only way forward. Because, guess what? You won't always get great sleep or feel well rested. There will be times you feel crappy. Sometimes the only solution is to take a mental step back, and say, "Okay, this is how it is right now." You don't actually need to do anything with unhelpful thoughts and feelings. They're just there. By allowing some flexibility, you keep from making a bad situation worse.

Sometimes the hardest thing about sleep is lying in the dark, alone with your own thoughts. But even when you are by yourself, it's important to remember that you're not alone. Other people are a key part of an upward spiral, and we'll cover that next.

Chapter 6

The Social Spiral

In case you hadn't noticed, humans don't have the same defenses as other animals. We're not particularly strong or fast. We don't have big teeth, sharp horns, or thick, leathery skin. Sure it's nice to have a big brain, but that can't get you very far on your own. The only way we survived in the wild was by relying on each other.

To keep humans close together, evolution utilized a neurotransmitter called *oxytocin*, which reduces stress and pain by making us feel connected to other people. Evolution also capitalized on existing circuitry for reward (the nucleus accumbens) and pain and fear (the limbic system), causing us to enjoy close relationships and to be scared and hurt by social rejection.

Unfortunately, in depression, the reactivity of these systems is a little bit off, making it harder to harness the joyful benefits of others and easier to experience the harsh negatives. This creates the potential for a downward spiral of loneliness and social isolation.

Fortunately, there are ways to modify our social circuits by both individual and social means. Most of this book has been focused on what you can do by yourself, but ultimately, it's very hard to overcome depression and be happy entirely on your own. Our brains just didn't evolve that way.

This chapter focuses on the power of other people to affect your brain and your mood in a myriad of ways, through physical contact, talking, or even just proximity. Your brain evolved to rely on other people, and this chapter will help you take advantage of that.

The Social Brain

Imagine you are an ancient human thirty thousand years ago wandering through the forest with your tribe. You see some berries off to the side and spend a couple minutes gathering them up. When you look up, you don't see anyone. They seem to have left you behind. You call out. No one responds. You are lost and alone in the deep, dark woods.

Thirty thousand years ago, being left alone might get you killed by a wild animal or eventually the elements, so your brain evolved to keep that from happening—by making it feel totally awful. It's understandable that your amygdala would be firing away and your hypothalamus would be on high alert.

It's also painful to experience social rejection—and the pain here is not a metaphor. The same pain circuits in your brain that get activated by a paper cut or by burning your hand on the stove—the anterior cingulate and insula—get activated by social rejection (Eisenberger, Jarcho, Lieberman, & Naliboff, 2006). And unfortunately, depression increases the brain's response to social rejection, showing more insula and amygdala reactivity (Kumar et al., 2017). In fact, having a brain that's more sensitive to rejection in parts of the anterior cingulate increases your risk of developing depression in the first place (Masten et al., 2011).

Now imagine that you're sitting at home by yourself, feeling a bit lonely, so you text your friend. She doesn't respond right away. You text another friend. Same thing. Now maybe one friend is in the shower, and maybe the other's phone battery died, but those alternative explanations probably don't pop into your head. It can feel like your friends have abandoned you.

The technology of communication has changed dramatically in the last thirty thousand years, but the human brain has not. Your brain still feels like you're being left alone in the forest. But while you are not actually in danger, depression can make it feel like you're always lost in the woods.

Recognizing your emotions and using words to describe them helps the prefrontal cortex soothe an overactive amygdala. How does the thought of being alone make you feel?

_____

_____

_____

_____

_____

_____

_____

Do you feel like your brain is more sensitive to social rejection? Can you think of a time you felt rejected, but it turned out there was a better explanation?

_____

_____

_____

_____

_____

_____

Loneliness and Social Isolation

Depression creates difficulties in the social spiral for two separate reasons: *loneliness* and *social isolation*. Loneliness is a feeling or perception: the longing to be close with others coupled with the fear of an unbridgeable gap. Social isolation, on the other hand, is a result of your behavior or your environment: you're just not around other people or you're not interacting with them.

It's possible to be alone without being lonely. For example, you could be sitting by yourself at home and still feel connected to your friends and family. Conversely, you could be at a party with friends and coworkers and still feel lost and alone. But, unfortunately, in depression, most people experience both loneliness and social isolation, and these two experiences reinforce each other in a downward spiral. The good news is that addressing either loneliness or social isolation creates the opportunity for an upward spiral.

Addressing Loneliness

A research group at the University of Chicago analyzed fifty published scientific papers on loneliness and found the three most effective solutions: create more opportunities for social contact, strengthen your social support, and deal with unhelpful thoughts about interactions and relationships (Masi, Chen, Hawkley, & Cacioppo, 2011). Part of addressing loneliness is dealing with social isolation, but creating a sense of connection depends on more than just having more social interactions: it requires more meaningful relationships.

Interestingly, through a combination of genetics and early childhood experiences, about 50 percent of feelings of loneliness are inherited from your parents. The other 50 percent is environmental, based on your current life circumstances (Masi et al., 2011). So some aspects of loneliness you can't control, but a large amount you do have some control over. Even the inherited part you have some control over, because some of that is about the types of habitual thinking you engage in about social interactions and relationships—and you can modify those types of thinking with practice.

People who are lonely are more likely to develop depression and to use negative social interactions as an excuse to isolate themselves (van Winkel et al., 2017). Because the limbic system gets amped up when it's out of control, it can sometimes feel calming to choose to be alone rather than worry about whether you can connect with others.

Have you noticed issues with loneliness or social isolation or both? What does loneliness feel like? Describe why you may not feel like being around other people. Are you aware of any unhelpful thoughts or beliefs that are contributing to feelings of loneliness or isolation? Recognizing your own tendencies and the feelings behind them can help give you insight into how to move forward.

_____

_____

_____

_____

The impulse to be alone is fully understandable, even reasonable. But it's not helpful as a habit, or to be alone for too long. Make the effort to keep interacting with others.

Taking Care of Yourself

When you aren't feeling very social, it can be very easy to let yourself go. After all, what's the point? No one is going to see you anyway.

Unfortunately, that creates the potential for a downward spiral. If you don't shower or brush your teeth, then you're less likely to want to interact with others, and it'll make it hard to break the cycle.

So, if you don't feel like being social, first take the steps to take care of yourself. Take actions that are consistent with or conducive to social interaction. It's much easier to interact with others if you shower regularly and brush your teeth.

Track Your Self-Care

Check off these basic self-care steps as you do them each day. Yes, it's easy to think that there's no point, but do them anyway. Feelings of pointlessness often pop into your head when you're depressed. Remember that they're just thoughts, and you don't have to do what they say.

	Mon	Tue	Wed	Thu	Fri	Sat	Sun	Mon	Tue	Wed	Thu	Fri	Sat	Sun
Take a shower														
Brush your teeth														
Get dressed														

Each day you do these activities, they'll get more strongly encoded in your dorsal striatum. This will help ensure that your positive actions won't have to always rely on willpower from your prefrontal cortex. On top of that, once you start checking off boxes, you'll stimulate dopamine release in the nucleus accumbens, helping to improve enjoyment and motivation.

Other self-care activities like the following help, too: .

☐ Get a haircut

☐ Get a manicure or pedicure

☐ Buy some new clothes

☐ Do your laundry

☐ Wash the dishes

☐ Make your bed

☐ Go to the dentist

☐ Go to the doctor

Add any other self-care activities that you can think of, and then choose the ones that matter to you, and add them to your activity-scheduling calendar that you started in chapter 2 or to your own calendar.

Being Around Other People

When you're sitting at home by yourself, it's much easier to get sucked into *rumination*, thinking the same negative thoughts over and over. Sometimes just being around other people can have a powerful effect. Both the hippocampus and striatum are sensitive to context, so changing your social context can change the emotions and habits that get triggered.

Are there times when you're stuck by yourself? Do you notice a tendency to ruminate? Where could you go as an alternative to being alone?

_____

_____

_____

_____

_____

When you're stuck in your own head, go somewhere to be with other people. It doesn't even matter if you interact with them or talk to them. Just being around others can be beneficial. Try going to a coffee shop, library, or the park.

Social Activities

Calling someone up to have a conversation can be a great source of social support, but social support can also be more informal. In fact, sometimes, conversations that arise organically as the result of a shared interest or activity can be the most helpful.

What are some activities that you enjoy that require you to be around other people? What activities that involve other people did you used to enjoy before you were depressed?

_____

_____

_____

_____

_____

_____

Use the activity-scheduling calendar from chapter 2 or your own calendar to schedule in some social activities.

Strengthening Social Support

Just because you think something doesn't make it true. Just because it feels like you're all alone doesn't mean you are. Depression insidiously makes you feel lonely and disconnected, often involving disrupted signaling of the neurotransmitter oxytocin, which normally helps you feel close and supported (McQuaid, McInnis, Abizaid, & Anisman, 2014).

Regardless of how it feels, there are likely many people in your life you can rely on for support—though you really need only one. Here are some steps to identify and strengthen your social support network, and to take advantage of the stress relief and enjoyment provided by the oxytocin system.

Identify Your Support Network

Who are the people you can rely on? They may include your parents, siblings, good friends, or coworkers. Just thinking about people who support you, or whom you feel connected to, decreases the brain's response to social exclusion (Karremans, Heslenfeld, van Dillen, & Van Lange, 2011).

1. Who appreciates you or thinks highly of you, whether or not you agree with them?

   _____

   _____

2. Who is there to help out if needed (e.g., a ride to the airport…)?

   _____

   _____

3. Who can you call, text, or visit for emotional support?

   _____

   _____

4. Who is good with giving you advice or helping you make decisions?

   _____

   _____

5. Who do you like spending time with?

   _____

   _____

6. Who can you do activities with?

   _____

   _____

You may rely on different people for different things or tend to rely on the same people for most things. If you can't think of anyone, that's okay too. There are many ways to take advantage of the social spiral, and you can utilize other methods from this chapter.

A Picture's Worth a Thousand Words

The striatum and hippocampus are sensitive to environmental cues. Take advantage of this to feel closer to others by making some small modifications to your surroundings. Put up pictures of people you care about and who care about you, or place in conspicuous spots other mementos that remind you of these people.

After you change your environment this way, note how it makes you feel. Do you notice a good feeling when you spot something that reminds you of someone you care about?

_____

_____

_____

_____

_____

Emotions about other people are complex, because even positive emotions can be mixed with sad nostalgia or longing or other negative emotions. Those negative emotions aren't bad; they often serve to remind you of who and what is important to you. Even if the people you care about are not around, you can still remember that they are a part of your life and who you are.

Using Your Support Network

Now that you have a better sense of who supports you and helps you feel better about yourself, how can you be in better touch? What gets in the way of reaching out?

_____

_____

_____

_____

_____

_____

It may have been a very long while since you called up someone to get together. This is not at all unlikely if you are depressed, and you may think that others don't want to hear from you. You may even think that they'd wonder, _Why the heck are you calling me?_

But have you ever had an old friend call you unexpectedly? Were you annoyed, or pleasantly surprised?

If you recognize that you were pleasantly surprised, don't you think others would be happy to hear from you? If not, then that's probably evidence of low self-esteem. Now there's nothing inherently wrong with low self-esteem. You don't need to focus on changing how you feel about yourself. It's hard to change your feelings directly. The problem is when your feelings affect your actions.

So if you're feeling down (or better yet, before you're feeling down), what's the best way to interact with your support network? The best thing to do is talk with the person in real life or meet up for an activity (Sherman, Michikyan, & Greenfield, 2013). The next best thing is talking on the phone, which is better than texts or emails. Seeing someone and hearing their voice activates your mirror neuron system in ways that texting can't match. Video chats can be a great solution, though Sherman et al. (2013) found that it really depends on your preferences: if you're not a fan of video chats, phone calls work better, but if you prefer video chats, then that's the better option.

Make the Call

Write down the names of three people who you enjoy talking to but haven't talked to in a few weeks, months, or even years.

- ☐ _____
- ☐ _____
- ☐ _____

Give them a call to catch up. If you feel awkward, you can always say, "We haven't talked in a while, and I just want to say hi, and see what's going on in your life." Check off their name after the call, but remember, you can always call again in the future.

Dealing With Negative Judgments

Do you find yourself annoyed when other people talk to you, or think they're probably full of themselves, or that they aren't worth talking to? That creates its own set of problems. The more critical you are of others, the more likely you are to feel that others are critical of you. That's because the medial prefrontal region that we use to understand our own mind is the same region used to understand other people's minds, and it's influenced by the emotional limbic system. Thus, one of the best ways to reduce your concern about the negative judgments and criticisms of other people is to reduce your own negative judgment and criticism.

Being judgmental can be especially damaging in close relationships, so it's helpful to be aware of it. Do you notice yourself being critical of others, particularly people you're close to? How does that impact how you feel about them or yourself?

_____

_____

_____

_____

_____

Often the things that bother us in other people are the same things that bother us about ourselves. Add a bit more kindness and compassion to how you treat yourself, and it will help in your relationships with others.

Put Your Phone Away

Do you check your cell phone frequently when you're with other people? That can unfortunately undermine the depth and quality of an interaction. Even having your cell phone sitting on the table, whether or not you check it, can disrupt a sense of closeness and trust (Przybylski & Weinstein, 2013). Keep your cell phone in your pocket or purse. Doing this will make it easier to have meaningful interactions.

Identifying Negative Social Influences

Sometimes the trigger for a negative mood is not an event but a person. Reversing the course of depression means not only spending more quality time with your support network but also reducing contact with the toxic people in your life.

Research shows that sometimes it can be beneficial to break social ties (Dingle, Stark, Cruwys, & Best, 2015). Other people reinforce our habits, including our social and emotional habits. So if you don't like those habits or the feelings those people trigger, change the people you surround yourself with.

Identify Toxic People

Answer the following questions to identify potential toxic people in your life, and consider reducing contact with them.

1. Which people in your life do you find it frustrating to interact with?

   _____

   _____

2. Who causes you to feel bad about yourself or think negative thoughts?

_____

_____

3. Could you reduce contact with this person (or these people)? How?

_____

_____

Feeling bad around other people does not necessarily mean that those people are bad—or toxic. Perhaps the feelings are caused not by something they are doing but rather by an unhelpful thought pattern you're having or something you'd like to change about yourself. If so, think of your interactions as an opportunity for personal growth. Otherwise, the best path forward is to get this person out of your life.

Unfortunately, it's not always possible to eliminate toxic people from your life, but just identifying them can make you more prepared. If you can predict how you'll react to being around them, it will be easier to remind yourself that it's just a feeling.

Resolving Conflicts

Since people have different goals and points of views, conflicts are inherent in relationships—even in great relationships. But because strong relationships are so important to the healthy functioning of the human brain, when we have a conflict with someone close to us, it can often cause a great deal of stress. To improve your relationships, you don't need to eliminate conflicts; you just need to get better at dealing with conflicts and reduce the stress they cause.

One of the biggest sources of stress is an unhelpful thought pattern called _emotional reasoning_. Emotional reasoning is a cognitive distortion that says if something feels true, then it must be true.

When someone does something that hurts us, it can often feel like they did it intentionally or that they don't care about our feelings. This may or may not be the case, because even though you're painfully aware of the impact of the other person's actions, you don't actually know their true intentions. Assuming that you know what's going on inside someone else's head is another common cognitive distortion called _mind reading_.

Our brains are so adept at trying to figure out other people's intentions and motivations that we often don't realize we're doing it. Your brain automatically uses the medial prefrontal cortex to figure out what someone else is thinking, but it doesn't treat its conclusions as a calculation or an assumption. It treats them as the truth!

For example, let's say your friend doesn't call you on your birthday. All you really know for sure is what your friend did—or didn't—do. You have no real idea why your friend did this, yet your assumptions about why are likely the whole reason you feel hurt.

When emotional reasoning and mind reading team up, it's easy to get stuck in conflicts. But if you can consciously recognize that you're making an assumption about the other person's intentions, then it may help you figure out what's really going on. This process is part of a set of cognitive tools called *reflective functioning*, which allows the prefrontal cortex to help calm a runaway limbic system.

Maybe your friend is a jerk and was trying to hurt you, but maybe he lost his cell phone, or maybe she broke her leg and had to go to the emergency room. More than likely, your friend was just too busy to call or simply forgot.

You don't need to know the answer. You just have to recognize that you are not a perfect mind reader, and be curious about possible other explanations. In the end, you might decide that your friend is, in fact, a jerk, but at least you'll have put some thought into it to come to that conclusion. Use the exercise below to disentangle a person's actions from your feelings, separating someone else's intentions from their impact on you.

Analyze a Conflict

Pick an unresolved conflict, argument, or situation with someone close to you that you're still angry or upset about. Describe the situation in a few sentences. What did the other person do or say? For now, just focus on the words or actions, and don't try to explain why it happened.

_____

_____

_____

_____

_____

Describe how the actions or words made you feel.

_____

_____

_____

_____

Going with your gut reaction, briefly state what you think the other person's intentions were. Why do you think he or she did or said this?

_____

_____

_____

Now see if you can come up with some other possible explanations for the words or actions (the intentions behind them). Maybe this person was busy, or tired, or upset about something, or even upset with you. Can you think of some other possible explanations for the behavior?

_____

_____

_____

_____

You don't have to know yet what the other person's true intentions were, or whether these intentions were reasonable. Sometimes just rethinking your assumptions will help you feel better about a situation, or at least have a clearer idea of why you're upset.

Sometimes rethinking your assumptions will facilitate a discussion with the other person. For more help with that, check out the book *Difficult Conversations: How to Discuss What Matters Most* (Stone, Patton, & Heen, 2010).

Unhelpful Thoughts in Relationships

Just as in other areas of your life, when you're deciding whether to go out or stay in, make new friends or keep to yourself, unhelpful thoughts may pop into your head that threaten to disrupt your full engagement with and enjoyment of other people. But if you can recognize them as unhelpful thoughts, then you can successfully prevent a downward spiral.

When it comes to relationships, our unhelpful thoughts can be particularly difficult to recognize. Here are a few examples of how unhelpful thoughts can crop up in relationships.

Unhelpful Thinking	Example
Predicting the future	*Hanging out with friends won't help me feel better.*
Selective attention	*You always cancel plans at the last minute,* or *You never listen to me.*
Black-or-white thinking	*She either likes me a lot or doesn't like me at all.*
Catastrophizing	*If my friends don't respond to my text messages right away, it means that they're angry with me or don't like me anymore.*

Examine Unhelpful Thinking

To help identify black-or-white thinking, write about a time when you were stuck wondering whether a relationship or situation was great or terrible. Can you elaborate on what was good and what was bad and start to add more nuance and shades of gray?

_____

_____

_____

_____

Now write about a time when you assumed the worst-case scenario—or a time when you thought you knew the future—and you turned out to be wrong.

_____

_____

_____

_____

Remind yourself of this the next time you make an assumption about how things will turn out.

What are some other unhelpful thoughts you have that increase your anxieties or stress about getting close with other people, doing activities with them, or talking to them? Are these thoughts true, partially true, or perhaps just plain wrong? Are they unlikely or unrealistic? How can you challenge these thoughts, accept them, or ignore them?

_____

_____

_____

_____

_____

The Physical Contact Spiral

Physical contact with other people releases oxytocin, which helps us feel closer to others and decreases stress (Grewen, Girdler, Amico, & Light, 2005). It's particularly true for prolonged physical contact, like a hug, or tender touches, like a gentle caress, or even brushing someone's hair. It may not be appropriate to go around hugging everyone, but shaking hands is generally okay.

Below is a list of ways to increase physical contact. Check off any that you feel comfortable with (with the caveat that in all physical contact, both people should feel fully comfortable) and add your own ideas:

- ☐ An extended hug

- ☐ A pat on the back

- ☐ Hugging hello

- ☐ Hugging good-bye

- ☐ Shaking hands

- ☐ A high five!

- ☐ Holding hands

- ☐ Kissing on the cheek

- ☐ Kissing on the lips

- ☐ Getting a massage (from a friend or a professional)

- ☐ Giving a massage

- ☐ Dancing with a partner

- ☐ Getting a haircut

- ☐ Getting a pedicure/manicure

- ☐ _____

- ☐ _____

- ☐ _____

- ☐ _____

Who can you make more physical contact with? Your spouse? Your children? Your friends? How can you be more physical?

_____

_____

_____

_____

_____

_____

_____

Asking for a hug from a friend might make you feel needy, but it's perfectly all right to be needy sometimes. It's also okay to offer to give someone a hug, particularly when they need support—and secretly, when you give a hug, you get one too.

The Sex Spiral

No discussion of physical contact can be complete without sex. Depression can lessen your sex drive, which often creates a downward spiral, particularly in intimate relationships. If you don't feel like having sex, it may make you withdraw from physical contact altogether. Your partner may feel hurt or abandoned, bringing more stress into the equation and making things more difficult. Don't forget to say "I love you."

If the physical intimacy has drained from your relationship, it's still possible to rekindle the flame. And you don't need to start with sex right away.

Try a massage or cuddling or holding hands. If you've drifted apart physically from your significant other, starting small is sometimes better than trying to force greater physical intimacy that you or your partner may be uncomfortable with.

The Generosity and Giving Spiral

In his inaugural address, President John F. Kennedy famously said, "Ask not what your country can do for you—ask what you can do for your country." Thinking about what you can do for others can be particularly difficult in depression, and yet that makes it all the more powerful.

You're probably reading this book with the hope that *you* will feel happier. But interestingly, that's often easier to approach indirectly, by focusing on others. Importantly, you don't have to feel generous in order to act generously. And when you stop focusing on your own situation and start focusing on helping others, it helps you too.

This is not to say that your problems aren't real and important. It's simply that focusing on your own problems is often not the best path forward. Focusing on compassion and on helping others is a great way to reverse the course of depression, because it activates the brain's reward system (Kim et al., 2009; Park et al., 2017). In fact, in many ways, your depression makes you the ideal candidate to help others. You know what it's like to suffer. There are others out there suffering in similar ways to you and also in dramatically different ways.

Below is a list of ways to be generous. Check off items that you might like to try, knowing that these are choices, not obligations. You can fill in the blanks with other ways to be generous:

☐ Make dinner for friends

☐ Buy or make a gift for a friend

☐ Give someone a compliment

☐ Volunteer at a nonprofit organization

☐ Donate to a worthy cause

☐ Participate in a fundraiser for a worthy cause

☐ Give someone a smile

☐ Give someone a word of encouragement

☐ Be a good listener

☐ Ask someone how you can help

☐ _____

☐ _____

☐ _____

What could you give to others? How could you benefit others or make their lives easier?

_____

_____

_____

_____

You can write down some of these actions in your activity-scheduling calendar from chapter 2 or in your own calendar. With other actions, you can be more spontaneous.

The Group Spiral

Humans evolved in tribes. We feel best when we belong. If you don't already have a place you feel like you belong, then join a group. Groups can not only help you feel better but also make you feel like you're more in control of your life (Greenaway et al., 2015). Joining a group helps reduce symptoms of depression and can even prevent it in the first place (Cruwys et al., 2013). And it unfortunately works the other way too: if you leave a supportive group, you can increase your risk for depression (Seymour-Smith, Cruwys, Haslam, & Brodribb, 2017).

Were there groups that you were a part of and active in before your depression?

_____

_____

If you didn't really have a good reason for leaving the group, try joining up again. And don't feel like you need to explain your absence. On the other hand, if you had good reasons for leaving the group, then it's probably for the best that the group is in your past. And now it's time to try joining a different group.

The key ingredient to utilizing the power of groups is feeling like you belong (Cruwys et al., 2014). Belonging is sometimes complicated, but you can help it along by joining groups of like-minded people who value what you value and enjoy what you enjoy. Alternatively, it can be easy if you join groups that your friends, family members, or coworkers are already a part of. That's a shortcut to belonging.

Sometimes belonging can feel like it's out of your control, because it seems like it's about what other people think of you. But in fact, belonging is a feeling inside you. You can help that along by contributing positively to the group and committing to its goals and values. Get more involved in the groups you're already a part of.

Below is a list of ways to belong to groups. Check off any that you might like to try, and add any others that you can think of:

☐ Join a sports league

☐ Attend the same pickup basketball game every week

☐ Sign up for a class (cooking, dancing, woodworking, creative writing…)

☐ Join a volunteer organization

☐ Attend a church

☐ Join others training for a triathlon, marathon, or walkathon

☐ Join a book club

☐ Join a card group

☐ Join an online group of people with similar interests

☐ Join a CrossFit gym

☐ Join a support group for depression (in person or online)

☐ Join the PTA or other school group

☐ _____

☐ _____

Pick a group and make plans to join. Mark your activity-scheduling calendar, and follow through.

The Canine Spiral

Other humans aren't the only beings that can help you take advantage of oxytocin and the social spiral. Humans have lived with domesticated dogs for thousands of years, and there's a neuroscientific reason for it. Dogs benefit your brain. If you're having difficulty connecting with other people, a dog can be the next best thing (sometimes even better).

Getting a dog has many benefits, from altering your habits to increasing the likelihood of positive social interactions. If you're sitting at home, but the dog wants to go for a walk, it's easier to find the motivation to get out of the house, because the dog is whining. Once you're on a walk, people are more likely to smile at you, or to strike up a casual conversation, if you have a dog.

Dogs can even modulate your oxytocin system in multiple ways. First, simply petting your dog can release oxytocin because of the soft, warm fur. Second, when your dog trusts you, just making eye contact releases oxytocin in you. Studies have shown that even being near a dog can reduce the negative feelings of social rejection (Aydin et al., 2012). Cats are a more complicated story, but if you're a cat person, there are fortunately many of the same benefits.

Below is a list of ways to interact with animals more. Check off any that you might like to try, and add any others that you can think of:

☐ Get a dog or cat

☐ Dog-sit or cat-sit for a friend

☐ Pet a friend's dog/cat

☐ Ask to pet dogs you pass on the street

☐ Go to a pet adoption and play with the animals

☐ Go horseback riding

☐ _____

☐ _____

Then put these activities in your activity-scheduling calendar, and do them.

Conclusion

Your brain evolved to connect with others, and utilizing that neural circuitry is one of the most powerful ways to create an upward spiral. It won't always happen all at once, but keep making small steps in the right direction.

And when you can't physically be with the people you care about and who care about you, even if you can't talk to them, it's still possible to feel close to them. You have in your brain a neural representation of the mind of everyone you're close with. Even someone who is no longer with you still exists in a very real way in the neural pathways and synaptic connections of your brain. You could have a conversation with them. You'd know how they would react. And the closer you are to them, the better you know them and the more accurate your representation of them is. So even when you're alone, the people in your life are in your brain.

If you still don't feel super connected to the important people in your life, or if you worry that there aren't enough important people in your life, that's okay. There's still more to come. Future chapters will focus on alternative strategies for feeling closer to others, such as mindfulness (chapter 8), gratitude (chapter 10), or self-compassion (chapter 10).

Chapter 7

The Goals and Decisions Spiral

You're stuck. Lost. Flailing. Paralyzed. Aimless. This is a common state of depression, when you're not making any clear progress toward important goals. It's both a cause of depression and a result.

Making decisions and pursuing goals both involve interactions of dopamine and serotonin in the brain stem, prefrontal cortex, and striatum (Rogers, 2011). When depressed, it's harder to create goals and act on them, because the brain is both indecisive and less responsive to rewards. Yet it's still possible to utilize this circuitry to create an upward spiral.

By allowing the prefrontal cortex to exert influence over the dorsal striatum, decisions and goals help you override unhelpful habits. Through top-down influence, they alter the way the brain processes and filters information, helping the limbic system ignore irrelevant details and focus on what matters. Lastly, goals and decisions enhance rewarding activity in the nucleus accumbens, making it easier to get excited and feel satisfied.

This process is complicated by the fact that there are likely many things that are important to you, and you're trying to get to all of them. This chapter will help you identify what's most important to you, which will simplify the decision-making process and fully harness the power of decision making.

Making Decisions

Decisions rely on many factors. They can come from careful consideration about possible options (relying on your prefrontal cortex) or from a gut feeling (relying on your limbic system and insula). These pathways are interrelated, and they affect each other. You can neither make decisions in a fully rational way, since your feelings about your decisions matter, nor make all your decisions on instinct, expecially when you're stressed or depressed, because every decision feels wrong. These decision-making regions must be in balance. So how can you help balance them?

Turn Down the Volume on Your Emotional Reactivity

The emotional limbic system and the stress response are primarily modulated by three forces: controllability, certainty, and consequences. The less control you have in a situation, the greater the limbic reactivity, and thus the greater intensity in your emotions. Similarly, more uncertainty and larger consequences also increase limbic reactivity. So how can you utilize this info when trying to make a decision?

Step 1. Focus on what you can control. You can't control other people. You can't control the past. Essentially the only things you can control are your actions in the present moment. You can't even control the overall outcome of a situation, except insofar as you have any control in the present moment. If you're having difficulty accepting this, you are not alone. This is one of the most difficult truths to accept. See chapter 8 for more information on this subject.

Step 2. Focus on what is certain. What or who are the steady features in your life? What will not change as a result of this decision?

Step 3. Focus on reducing perceived consequences. Put the decision in context. What are the actual consequences? Are you engaging in any unhelpful thinking patterns? Often your own critical feelings toward yourself increase your perception of negative consequences. Practicing more self-compassion will simplify the decision-making process, because often the biggest negative consequence to a decision is your own harsh self-criticism (see chapter 10).

Utilize the Upward Spiral

Reducing stress and improving your mood can simplify the decision-making process. What's the best way to do that? Utilize the upward spiral. You've already read more than half a book about it.

Take a few deep breaths to lower your stress response. Call up a friend and chat—you could ask for advice or just reconnect. Go for a run. Sleep on it—everything feels better in the morning. Continue reading this book and learn how to apply mindfulness or gratitude strategies to the decision-making process.

What are your favorite ways to reduce stress?

_____

_____

_____

_____

_____

_____

Getting some perspective can also help. Thinking about what is most important to you (or clarifying your values) helps reduce the stress response in difficult situations (Creswell et al., 2005).

Thinking About What's Important

What is important to you in the different parts of your life? What kind of person do you want to be? For example, in family life, what do you value most? Being a good parent or a loving spouse, or something else? In work and career, do you put getting ahead or getting along with your colleagues first? For each part of life that you value, write about what's most important to you.

Parts of Life	What's Most Important to You
Family	
Friendships and community	
Romantic relationships	
Work/career	
Education, personal growth, and development	
Recreation	
Spirituality/religion	
Health and physical well-being	

Now take a moment to think about the relative importance of these parts of your life. Which ones stand out above the rest? Which ones do you care less about? Put a circle around the one or two parts of your life that are most important to you. Focusing on your values, and remembering what's most important, will help you set goals and make decisions.

Happiness Is Not a Helpful Goal

Happiness for its own sake can feel meaningless and thus work against itself. On top of that, happiness is too abstract to be a useful goal. Happiness is not a place you get to; it's a result of your actions, your goals, and your values all lining up.

Think about why you want to be happy. What important things or important people is your depression getting in the way of? How can you work toward what's important to you even if you're depressed?

Figuring out what's important to you or clarifying your values helps give you direction, but your values can sometimes be too abstract to act on. Goals help make values more concrete and actionable, which facilitates the release of dopamine. A value is like wanting to drive across the country and having some vague notion that you want to go west. A goal means turning that into something specific and achievable, so you can take action—a route to follow. So the initial goal might be to head toward Denver, which means the first actionable step is to get on Interstate 70.

So let's say it's important to me to be a good father—that's a value. A goal in line with that might be to pay more attention to my kids. I make that actionable by making a plan to not check my email when I'm with my kids. Values provide direction, but creating goals consistent with those values and breaking those down into actionable steps will help you get somewhere meaningful.

Defining Your Values and Goals

Looking at the preceding list, think about the two or three things that are most important to you at this point in your life. What values do these things represent?

_____

_____

_____

_____

_____

Can you point to certain goals that will help move you in the direction of your values?

_____

_____

_____

_____

What goals were important to you before you got depressed? Are these goals still important to you? If so, can you still work toward them? How could you take a concrete step?

_____

_____

_____

_____

_____

What actions can you take right now that will move you toward your goals?

_____

_____

_____

_____

Decide by Love, Not Fear

In every decision, we have the opportunity to be guided by what we want or what we don't want—what we love or what we fear. While fear is unpleasant, it acts as a great spotlight to help identify what's important to you. For any statement you can make about what you're scared of, there's a complementary statement to make about what's important to you. For example, "I'm scared that people I'm close to will leave me." That could be rephrased in the positive as "It's important to me to be close with people." Both statements could lead to a decision about what to do next, but they don't usually lead you to the same decision.

For example, if I'm scared of people leaving me, I might try to protect myself by deciding (not necessarily consciously) to avoid close relationships in the first place. This decision made from fear would actually make it less likely to get what's important to me: a close relationship.

Deciding to move toward an important goal is scary, because failure is always a possibility. But focusing on the joy of success, rather than the fear of failure, will help keep you from getting stuck. You just need to convince yourself that your goal is more important than what your fear.

Fears vs. Values

Use the left column to write down an outcome that keeps coming to mind as something you don't want to happen (something you're scared of happening). Then reframe each of these fears or worries as something you do want to happen. (Change "If I do X, I'll miss out on Y" to "If I do X, I'll get all the wonderful things that come with it.")

What I don't want to happen	What is important to me
Example: *I don't want to lose my job.*	*I want to keep my job. I like my job, and it's important to me.*

Decide on Value, Not Cost

Let's say I'm trying to buy a car. I could look at the sticker price and decide, *Wow, that's way too much to pay for a car.* But does that mean I shouldn't buy the car? Well, there are two parts to the equation: what it costs and what you get. The more you focus on what it will cost, the harder it is to acquire anything of value.

Anything of value will always cost something—a monetary cost, a time cost, an effort cost, a risk cost. But if you always judge things based on what they cost, then it's very hard to get what you want, because it will almost always cost a lot.

In depression, it can feel like everything costs a lot. Everything is difficult and requires so much energy. If you're feeling stuck making a decision that you think is good, write down all the benefits. Focus on the value, not the cost.

Think of a tough decision where you think you know your preference but are having trouble following through. List the benefits of making this decision, and let them sink in.

_____

_____

_____

_____

_____

_____

Are those benefits important to you? If yes, is there another way to get those benefits? If no, then even though it's difficult, the path is clear before you.

Don't Try to Make the "Best" Decision

The French writer Voltaire wrote that "the best is the enemy of the good." If you're always aiming for the best or the perfect decision, then it's easy to get stuck.

This might seem counterintuitive, but when you're stuck, don't try to make the best decision. Just make a good decision. In other words, don't try to be your happiest—just try to be happy.

People who always try to make the best decisions are called *maximizers*, and they tend to have higher levels of depression. Maximizing correlates over time with decreased positive emotions and increased negative emotions (Bruine de Bruin, Parker, & Strough, 2016). The relationship between maximizing and depression is driven by the tendency to search for the best decision, even when it's not possible, and to keep looking for alternatives even when you've found something good.

Importantly, this is not the same thing as having high standards. It is okay to have a high standard of excellence—that doesn't increase depression. Accepting good enough does not mean that you have to lower your standards. It simply means that good enough is good enough.

If you can think about your decision briefly and easily determine the best choice, then great. Go for it. But often, there is no best decision. Each and every decision has advantages and drawbacks. It is one of those realities of life we must all learn to accept—in the same way we must learn to accept incomplete control. While there are always pluses and minuses involved in a decision, no one else can tell you what's more important. You have to choose for yourself.

When a decision is difficult, it means that there are many things that are important to you. If only one thing were important, then decisions would be easy. You can't get everything you want, but at least you can move toward what's most important.

What is the most important feature of the decision in front of you? What would a good enough outcome look like?

_____

_____

_____

_____

_____

_____

Decision-Making Strategies

People with depression tend to use fewer adaptive decision-making strategies and more maladaptive ones (Alexander, Oliver, Burdine, Tang, & Dunlop, 2017). *Adaptive decision-making* simply means you're clear about what your objective is in the decision and you're aware of the options. There are three main maladaptive strategies: hypervigilance, buck passing, and procrastinating.

Maladaptive Decision Making

Here are examples of the three main maladaptive decision-making strategies. In the third column, check off any of the maladaptive strategies that you've noticed yourself engaging in.

Decision-Making Strategy	Example	Strategies You Use
Hypervigilance	*I'm so worried that something could go wrong that I make rushed or impulsive decisions, often contradicting my previous decisions.*	
Buck passing	*I'd prefer to have someone else make the decision for me, so it's not my fault.*	
Procrastinating	*I often put off making a decision to the last minute or until it's too late.*	

There's no use in getting angry at yourself for using maladaptive strategies—just start using an adaptive strategy more often. Therapies that focus on improved decision making have been proven effective at alleviating depression (Barth et al., 2013). Here's a recipe for making decisions using an adaptive strategy (Leykin, Roberts, & DeRubeis, 2011).

Adaptive Decision Making

Step 1. Brainstorm. Think about a decision you have to make. In the first column of the table, list all the options that may be realistic to choose from. For now, don't worry about whether these are good options or not. Just list all the possibilities.

Realistic Options	Ranking

Step 2. Rank these options. Number your options by putting a 1 next to your favorite, and continuing (2, 3, 4, and so on) down to your least favorite. Are you satisfied with your favorite choice? If so, great! You're done. If not, then continue to step 3.

Step 3. Filter. Look at your first and second options. Write them down in the space provided. Then, comparing those two options, list the pros and cons of each one.

Option 1:		Option 2:	
Pros for Option 1	**Cons** for Option 1	**Pros** for Option 2	**Cons** for Option 2

Step 4. Decide or rethink. Considering the two options you've examined, would you change your mind about the order in which you've ranked them or not? Whichever you decide, congratulations, you've made your choice!

Focus on Action, Not Feelings

We have this amazing prefrontal cortex that can see the future and everything that could possibly go wrong. That can be a blessing when it helps us avoid negative outcomes. But if you get stuck in a spiral of worrying and indecisiveness, it can also be a curse.

While worrying can actually help momentarily reduce anxiety, it is not an effective long-term solution, because worries are focused on thoughts and feelings, not actions. Without action, you're stuck. To move forward, you don't need to stop worrying; you just need to respond to your worrying with some concrete action. While worrying activates more self-focused aspects of the prefrontal cortex, planning activates the parts of the prefrontal cortex more closely connected to the action centers in the brain (that is, the striatum).

Furthermore, when it comes to decision making, most people persist in thinking about the issue until they feel good about making the decision. But that's often too high a bar, particularly if you're depressed. When you're depressed, generally no amount of thinking is going to magically make you feel great.

That's why the most important component of decision making is action. If you're stuck in a place, and you don't know where to go, you've got to start moving somewhere. Sure, sitting there and getting your bearings may help you realize the right way to go, but if that doesn't work, then you're just wasting time. What's the solution? Pick a direction and start moving.

Your actions have the ability to alter the future. What's one thing you could do right now that would have a positive impact or at least move you closer to making a decision?

_____

_____

_____

_____

_____

Another way to deal with worries is to make concrete plans for potential future scenarios: if-then plans. *If X happens, then I'll do Y.* This is like a coach making a game plan for the team or a military general preparing for battle. You can't always know what the future will throw at you, but if you have a plan in place to deal with different scenarios, then you will be much better prepared.

Planning for Worries

What are some things that you worry about, and what could you do if they happened? List your worries in the column on the left, and then write down some actions you could take if these things were to happen.

Worry	Action Plan

Focus on One Thing at a Time

Sometimes one goal gets in the way of another goal. If both goals are important, they can pull you in different directions, and you feel stuck. That's fine. Most people have many things that are important to them. But instead of doing two things at once half-heartedly, put your whole heart into one thing, and then put your whole heart into the other.

Sometimes there's a good reason to pick one goal over the other. Other times there's no good reason. You just have to choose. Sometimes the hardest decisions are the ones that really don't matter.

Research has shown that multitasking actually gets in the way of productivity. Trying to do multiple things at once or switching back and forth frequently between tasks actually makes you less productive and less satisfied with the work you're doing (Etkin & Mogilner, 2016). Pick one goal or task to work on now, and devote your full focus and effort on it. Then do the next task.

Completing Small Tasks

Write down a series of tasks that you've been putting off. The order doesn't really matter. Now start with the first task.

To stay focused, give yourself a time limit and set a timer. Think of it as a game, a race against the clock. When you complete the task, even if you went overtime, give yourself a check mark, which will provide a dopamine boost. If you have time, go on to the next task. If not, then come back to this list later, and accomplish more.

Small Task	Time Limit	Completed

Setting Goals

Generally, our actions are determined by how we feel in the moment. If you feel like eating, you eat. If you feel like working, you work. But that's a real problem if you're depressed, because generally you don't feel like doing anything—at least not anything helpful.

This is where setting some goals can be powerful. Goals can actually change the way you feel, but they have to be clear and concrete, and you have to take action.

Goals help the brain organize information, allowing the prefrontal cortex to send out clearer directives and increase motivation. Goals also tell the nucleus accumbens what to respond to when you accomplish something, so making progress toward your goals and meeting them becomes more enjoyable and rewarding.

Mark Your Calendar

One of the best ways to start doing stuff is to put it on your calendar. It changes the default. If you want to hang out with someone, then instead of going back and forth wondering about times, go ahead and suggest a time and then pencil it in on your calendar. That makes the plan real. You can use the activity-scheduling calendar from chapter 2 or your own calendar.

Along similar lines, making a to-do list helps to motivate you. Making a to-do list counteracts a tendency that you may have to make goals that are amorphous and poorly defined. And it's perfectly fine to put some things on there that you've recently completed—like "Make a To-Do List"!

Tasks on your to-do list should be concrete and accomplishable. Concrete means that at some point in the future, you could check off the task as being completed. Accomplishable means that you can feel confident you can make meaningful progress in a short amount of time. If an item does not seem concrete, then define it more precisely. If it does not seem accomplishable, then break it down into smaller steps that are more easily accomplished.

Break It Down

Start by setting small goals, ones that you know you can achieve. Completing a task, even a tiny task, causes release of dopamine in the nucleus accumbens. Therefore, achieving a small goal will give you a sense of progress and completion. And to make large goals more manageable, it's helpful to think of them as a series of small goals.

Meeting Your Goal

Think of a big goal that is overwhelming to you but that you would like to accomplish in the next week or over the next month, and then take these steps to break it down into smaller parts, so you can meet it.

Name the goal here: _____

Now break this goal down into a series of smaller goals, or tasks that you would need to do to meet the bigger goal.

Task 1. _____

Task 2. _____

Task 3. _____

Task 4. _____

Task 5. _____

Are each of these smaller goals accomplishable, or do you need to break any of them down further?

Task 1 steps: _____

_____

_____

_____

Task 2 steps: _____

_____

_____

_____

Task 3 steps: _____

_____

_____

_____

Task 4 steps: _____

_____

_____

_____

Task 5 steps: _____

_____

_____

_____

What are some steps you could take in the next hour to begin working toward your goal for the next week or month? (Note: I'm giving you only two lines here for a reason. Don't try to do everything at once.)

1. _____

2. _____

Use this exercise as a to-do list for accomplishing your goal. Give yourself a gold star (or at least a check mark) for completing each step toward your goal.

Focus on Effort

When it comes to starting your pursuit of goals, particularly bigger ones, it's more helpful to focus on effort than on completion. The outcome is not always under your full control, and that can be stressful and demotivating. But your effort is under your control. Once you get some momentum toward a goal, then you can focus on finishing to get an extra boost of dopamine.

One of the most effective methods for focusing on effort is the pomodoro technique. It was invented by an Italian guy named Francesco Cirillo, who had an alarm clock shaped like a tomato, so the technique is named after the Italian word for tomato: *pomodoro*. The following exercise uses his technique.

E Is for Effort

Think of a huge project that you would like to get done. (This can be the goal that you outlined in the previous exercise.) Think of a clear step to take toward that goal, and commit to just doing that. Set a timer for twenty-five minutes, and work. Twenty-five minutes is long enough to make meaningful progress—and short enough to make all your excuses pretty much bogus. No, you don't have to check your email. It can wait. No you don't need to eat something—you won't starve.

The amount of progress you make is irrelevant. Success is simply defined by working for twenty-five minutes. When the timer goes off, give yourself a pat on the back—and a check mark on a piece of paper to make it tangible. You did it! Take a five-minute break to relax and enjoy yourself. Repeat three to four times in a row before taking a longer break (thirty to sixty minutes). It might sound like a silly technique, but that's how I got through writing most of this book.

Buy a Ticket

Imagine you could take a trip anywhere in the world. You could go to Paris or Tokyo or Machu Picchu, or sit on a beach drinking mai tais on a tropical island. The possibilities can be thrilling or overwhelming. But regardless, you can't get excited about specifics until you pick a place.

Should you start brushing up on your French or your Japanese? Should you buy a new raincoat or sunglasses? You can't make any of these choices, or get excited about any of them, until you take a concrete step toward a plan.

It's easy to understand excitement in terms of roulette. In roulette, you can't really get excited about any of the numbers until you place a bet. This is how decisions, goals, commitments, and consequences mediate enjoyment and loss. Once you actually place a bet and things are in motion, you will start to feel more emotions and sensations. They will not always feel good. But this is called living.

To feel the excitement, you actually have to take action toward a specific goal. You can think of this as throwing your knapsack over the wall, a concept popularized by psychologist Tal Ben-Shahar: once all your stuff is on the other side of the wall, then you've got no choice but to get yourself over. You're committing yourself to finding a way, and your brain treats that very differently from when you're in the evaluation phase. When you make progress toward a goal, dopamine gets released in the nucleus accumbens to continue motivating you. But you've got to take the first step. Actions speak louder than words, particularly to yourself.

So how do you make a decision real to yourself? Buy a ticket. Put it on your calendar. Put it on your to-do list. Put up a reminder in your personal space (in your bedroom or at work). Buy a book about it. Tell a friend about your plan. Sign up for it. Ask someone to do it with you. Or anything else to make it more than just a thought you can ignore—make it real!

Avoid "Supposed to," "Have to," and "Should"

What's the quickest way to suck the fun out of something? Make it mandatory. Whenever you catch yourself thinking you're *supposed to* do something—or that you *have to* or *should* do it—and find the thought demotivating, try to rephrase it.

Reframing Should-Thoughts

Fill in the column on the left with *should-thoughts* that you make to yourself or thoughts that include the words "have to" or "supposed to." Then in the column on the right, reframe them with accurate descriptions.

Should-Thoughts	Reframing with Accurate Descriptions
Example: *I should be more motivated about exercising.*	*I want to feel more motivated about exercising.*
Example: *I have to improve my sleep hygiene or I won't have any energy.*	*I want to improve my sleep hygiene because I like having more energy.*

Should-Thoughts	Reframing with Accurate Descriptions

Once you stop thinking about what you're supposed to do, it will be easier to uncover what you want to do, and often they're the same thing.

Be Your Best Possible Self

There are times when it is helpful to think about the best possible outcome—not when it comes to a stressful decision but when it comes to envisioning your future. Writing about your best possible self has been shown to help deal with trauma, improve mood, and decrease depressive symptoms (Loveday, Lovell, & Jones, 2016). Even though the exercise is brief, some of these effects can last for several months.

This exercise is effective because it utilizes the prefrontal cortex to imagine how everything could go right (Luo, Chen, Qi, You, & Huang, 2018). While this is more difficult for some people than others, that makes it all the more important to practice.

Imagining Yourself at Your Best

Think about your life six months from now. Imagine that everything has gone as well as it possibly could. You have worked hard and succeeded at accomplishing your goals. Think about what it feels like and what you did to get there. Now, set a timer for ten minutes and write about what you imagined.

_____

_____

_____

_____

_____

_____

_____

_____

_____

_____

_____

_____

_____

_____

_____

_____

Conclusion

What if it doesn't feel comfortable to set goals? Well, of course it won't feel comfortable. But doing what feels comfortable is following the striatum, and that's what is keeping you stuck. Fortunately you don't always have to listen to your striatum, even if it's shouting. You can make a new choice.

Think about what's important to you. Set a big goal to inspire yourself. Too overwhelmed? Set a super small goal.

Don't try to do everything at once. Take one small step at a time. Make a decision, set a specific goal, and take action to move toward it. That's how great things are accomplished. That's how you've been making your way through this book—and look, you're two-thirds through it! That's how your upward spiral will continue.

Chapter 8

The Mindfulness and Acceptance Spiral

In one of my favorite dragon-based TV shows, Daenerys Targaryen, the mother of dragons, wants to rush off to war but is counseled that it could make things worse. She feels very anxious and wants to do something to fix the situation. She asks her advisor, "So what would you have me do?"

He responds, "Nothing. Sometimes nothing is the hardest thing to do."

Most of this book is about things you can do to help yourself feel better. But the difficult truth is that sometimes, you can't do anything. In fact, trying to always fix your emotions can just make you feel worse. You can't fix your emotions, because your emotions aren't broken. Always trying to fix how you're feeling, instead of learning to be okay with your feelings, is itself part of the problem.

Learning to accept negative feelings is a powerful way to combat the negativity of depression, because it allows you to act intentionally rather than be entirely guided by your moment-to-moment feelings. That does not mean accepting that things should be this way; it means accepting that they are this way.

Acceptance of the present moment facilitates mindfulness, and vice versa. Mindfulness is a process of guiding your attention to something specific instead of being a slave to wherever your attention happens to wander. Part of that process is simply recognizing the fact that your attention has wandered and gently guiding it back. This modifies communication between the prefrontal cortex and the limbic system in ways that help prevent a downward spiral.

This chapter is not about doing something to fix your feelings. It's about guiding your attention and learning to be okay with being in the present moment. And while sometimes that's the hardest thing to do, it's often the most powerful.

Acceptance

A yoga teacher once said something that really stuck with me: "Clear boundaries, infinite freedom." Once you accept what you cannot do, and what you cannot control, then it frees you up to focus on the things that you can do something about. Once you accept your limitations, then they stop being so limiting.

Importantly, acceptance is not the same thing as resignation. Resignation is a judgment that you don't like where things are or where they're headed, but you've given up trying to change them. By contrast, acceptance is a nonjudgmental acknowledgment of where you are.

Take the following sentence and read it in an exasperated voice: "I don't like being in this situation, and it feels like I'll never get out of it!" Try it in a resigned voice or with any other negative emotion. Now read that same sentence but without any emotion, like you're just stating a fact: "I don't like being in this situation, and there is nothing I can do about it." That's acceptance.

Acceptance and the Brain

One of the prefrontal cortex's main jobs is to try to control stressful situations. And when you believe that you have control over a stressful event, your brain releases norepinephrine to help organize a response. But what if it's something you can't control?

In one particular study of uncontrollable stress, the less subjects felt like they had control over their lives, the more activity they had in cognitive control parts of the prefrontal cortex (Wiech et al., 2006). Lack of acceptance means continuing to try to control the things that you can't control, like negative feelings.

But once you stop trying to control a stressor, then the prefrontal planning regions can disengage from it. You're no longer stuck in a battle you can't win. You're not retreating—you're regrouping. It actually helps to reduce stress. In fact, people with higher acceptance also have higher heart rate variability, which corresponds to a reduced fight-or-flight stress response (see chapter 4) (Visted et al., 2017). Acceptance of negative emotions also increases activity in emotional prefrontal regions that help to regulate the emotional limbic system (Salomons, Johnstone, Backonja, Shackman, & Davidson, 2007). Letting go of your desire to control negative events may not sound like the best plan, but letting go can be extremely powerful, depending on the situation.

When it comes to something that is uncontrollable, letting go of trying to control it is not giving up—it is acceptance. Because regardless of whether you accept it, it's still there. Acceptance just allows you to stop banging your head against the same wall.

But keep in mind that it's also not helpful to accept something that actually is controllable. If you're in a problematic relationship or in a job that you don't like, acceptance is not always the best path. Often the best solution is to fix the situation: work on the relationship or break up with the person, ask for changes at your job to improve working conditions or find a new job, and so on.

The problem arises when trying to fix things is the only way you approach your problems, because at some point you will run into something, like negative emotions, that can't be fixed. They are not controllable. What do you do then? You need to learn to accept them. Mindfulness can help.

What Is Mindfulness?

Many people confuse mindfulness with meditation, but mindfulness and meditation are not the same. Meditation is one means of practicing mindfulness, but there are many other ways to practice it. Mindfulness is not about what you're doing but about how you're doing it. It's a process of directing your attention to the present moment, which includes your physical, mental, and emotional experiences.

Imagine you take a glass of water and swish it around. If you stop momentarily, the water will still be swirling around. To stop the water from swirling, should you swish the glass in the other direction? No, in fact, if you do this, you will likely add to the problem. It's best to simply put down the glass and stop trying to fix the problem. The less you try to take action to fix it, the more the water will settle down. The same is true of the thoughts and feelings swirling through your brain. Letting them be is often the best approach. But why is doing this so important?

The Benefits of Mindfulness on the Brain and Body

Practicing mindfulness has been demonstrated to reduce anxiety, stress, and depression, improve well-being, and even enhance clear thinking (Goldberg et al., 2017; Fledderus, Bohlmeijer, Pieterse, & Schreurs, 2012). Mindfulness has such widespread benefits because it affects so many different neural circuits.

The primary regions influenced by mindfulness practices are the prefrontal cortex, anterior cingulate cortex, and the insula (Tang, Hölzel, & Posner, 2015; Young et al., 2018). The striatum can also be affected. Just a week of mindfulness practice enhances activity in both emotional and cognitive parts of the prefrontal cortex, as well as the anterior cingulate and insula (Zeidan, Martucci, Kraft, McHaffie, & Coghill, 2014). This means increased emotional regulation, impulse control, and awareness of the present moment. And even briefer effects are possible. For example, some changes in neural pathways in the anterior cingulate are visible after just a few hours (Posner,

Tang, & Lynch, 2014). These changes reflect the strengthening of particular neural pathways, an example of neuroplasticity.

Mindfulness…

- **Reduces emotional reactivity.** Simply becoming aware of your emotions allows the prefrontal cortex to calm the amygdala's automatic reactivity (Lieberman et al., 2007). And over time, the prefrontal cortex gets better at soothing the amygdala, reducing the intensity of overwhelming emotions (Gotink, Meijboom, Vernooij, Smits, & Hunink, 2016).

- **Strengthens reward circuits.** The brain has a tendency to swing between excitement and disappointment, with disappointment leading to a drop in pleasurable nucleus accumbens activity (Kirk & Montague, 2015). These wild swings create the potential for a downward spiral, but mindfulness training helps smooth out those jagged swings.

- **Elevates mood.** Mindfulness training has been shown to improve mood and depressive symptoms (Goldberg et al., 2017; Winnebeck, Fissler, Gärtner, Chadwick, & Barnhofer, 2017). A large analysis of several studies found that mindfulness-based interventions are just as effective as other forms of treatment for depression (Strauss, Cavanagh, Oliver, & Pettman, 2014).

- **Reduces stress.** Mindfulness has measurable effects on heart rate, blood pressure, mood, and anxiety (Zeidan, Johnson, Gordon, & Goolkasian, 2010). This illustrates how the mind and attention can influence your body. It might be stressful sometimes, as you become aware of feelings you were trying to suppress, but by acknowledging and accepting them, you can actually reduce the stress hormone cortisol in stressful situations (Lindsay, Young, Smyth, Brown, & Creswell, 2018).

- **Changes bad habits.** Mindfulness has been shown to help change bad habits like smoking and other addictions (Goldberg et al., 2017). Bad habits tend to be almost involuntary, with the urge to act followed immediately and automatically by the action. Mindfulness helps to create a breath of space to help replace bad habits with more intentional actions.

- **Improves clear thinking.** Mindfulness training improves clear thinking and even mental performance on difficult tests (Mrazek, Franklin, Phillips, Baird, & Schooler, 2013). Importantly, the effect is strongest for the people who are the most distractible at the start.

- **Prevents relapse.** Mindfulness training has been shown to greatly decrease the chance of relapse (Kuyken et al., 2016). This effect is strongest in people with the worst depression. So if you're climbing out of depression, mindfulness can help keep you from sliding back.

Which of these benefits of mindfulness are most important to you and why?

_____

_____

_____

_____

_____

What Mindfulness Isn't

There are many ways that your practice of mindfulness can go astray, and many of these problems arise from a misunderstanding of what mindfulness is. Read the following statements about what mindfulness isn't, and respond to the question that follows by checking the box "yes" or "no."

- Mindfulness is not clearing your mind of all thoughts and feelings. You cannot control your automatic thoughts and feelings, and you shouldn't try to. Mindfulness may lead to a quieting of your thoughts, but you can't force that to happen. You simply have to allow it to happen.

  Are you trying to force your mind to clear?   Yes ☐   No ☐

- Mindfulness is not relaxation. It is often relaxing, but that's not the goal. Relaxation is also helpful in depression, but it benefits you in a distinct way from mindfulness.

  Are you trying hard to relax?   Yes ☐   No ☐

- Mindfulness is not about suppressing your feelings. It's about becoming aware of the things you're feeling instead of trying to change or ignore them.

  Are you trying to suppress unpleasant feelings?   Yes ☐   No ☐

- Mindfulness is not positive thinking. Focusing on the positive aspects of reality has many benefits for mood and stress that are covered in chapter 10, but those are distinct from mindfulness.

  Are you trying to focus on the positive?   Yes ☐   No ☐

- Mindfulness is not wallowing or ruminating. Mindfulness is about immersing yourself in the present moment, while wallowing and ruminating focus on past mistakes and how they'll continue to haunt you into the future. Mindfulness includes noticing the brain's judgmental thoughts but without getting carried away by them.

Are you wallowing or ruminating?   Yes ☐   No ☐

If you said yes to any of the above questions, do you feel like a failure?   Yes ☐   No ☐

If you said yes to any of the above questions, including the last one, that doesn't mean you're a failure. You just became aware of what you were feeling or thinking. Mindfulness asks you to continue on in that manner. If you're being judgmental, just acknowledge your judgment. The recognition of your thoughts and feelings in the present moment automatically brings your focus to the present moment.

Keys to Mindfulness

Being present means guiding your focus to the present moment. In other words, you pay attention to something that's happening right now and don't pay attention to what's not happening right now.

It takes a lot of concentration to stay present, since we're often ruminating on the past or projecting ourselves into some catastrophic future. But with practice, we can get better.

Enhanced awareness of the present moment is reflected by increased activity in the insula as we actually start to feel our emotions (Young et al., 2018). When we're not so caught up in what might or might not happen in the future, we are left free to fully experience the present.

One of the obstacles to paying specific attention to something is that we often get distracted by a thought or emotion. That's okay. You do not have to avoid distraction, but once you realize that your attention has wandered, with mindfulness, you just guide it back to where you want your focus to be.

One strategy to decrease the distracting nature of emotions is simply to identify them. Identifying an emotion automatically brings your attention to the present, because it is something you are feeling right now. Furthermore, this small act of self-awareness allows the prefrontal cortex to calm the amygdala's automatic reactivity (Lieberman et al. 2007). This can reduce the intensity of the emotion.

Stop reading for a moment and ask yourself, *What emotions am I feeling right now?* Write them down here.

_____

_____

_____

_____

In guiding your attention to your emotions, you may have noticed an automatic judgment about your emotional experience and tried to fix it. This happens all the time while practicing mindfulness. Again, there's nothing actually wrong with these automatic judgments. You don't need to stop your judgmental thoughts. In fact you can't—that's just the limbic system doing its job. With mindfulness, your job is to simply become aware of your judgmental thoughts. Once you recognize and acknowledge them, you can either keep attending to them if you like or gently guide your attention back to whatever you were paying attention to before your thoughts interrupted you.

Putting Mindfulness into Practice

Mindfulness can be tough, because we're so used to being mindless. In fact, if given the choice between sitting quietly with your thoughts or getting an electric shock, most people would prefer the shock (Wilson et al., 2014).

You can be mindful in anything that you do or even while doing nothing. It's a way of being, not an action. But it is something you can practice, like playing soccer or the piano. You can't perfect it, but by working on it, you can get better at it. Here are some ways to practice mindfulness.

This first exercise was adapted from the work of a psychologist consulting for NASA (Joiner, 2017).

Graphing Your Mood

Notice your mood over the next five minutes by graphing it on a negative mood chart. On the left is a scale of 1 to 10, where 10 means feeling terrible and 1 means feeling good. Describe your mood right now at time 0:00 by putting a small X at the appropriate point on the scale. Then set a timer for five minutes. After thirty seconds elapses, add another X to represent your mood, and continue to add an X after every thirty seconds until time is up. Connect the Xes to observe how your mood shifted over time. Your goal of this exercise is not to change your mood but to just observe it.

Negative Mood Chart (Scale of 1 to 10)

	0:00	0:30	1:00	1:30	2:00	2:30	3:00	3:30	4:00	4:30	5:00
10											
9											
8											
7											
6											
5											
4											
3											
2											
1											
Time	0:00	0:30	1:00	1:30	2:00	2:30	3:00	3:30	4:00	4:30	5:00

Did your mood improve? If so, recognize that when you're feeling bad, you don't need to do anything but just allow your mood to change on its own.

Did your mood stay the same? At least it didn't get worse.

Did your mood change a lot? If so, it's important to recognize that moods, feelings, emotions, and thoughts are transient. You don't need to do anything about them. You can often just wait them out.

Did your mood get worse? If so, were you slipping into rumination or getting anxious about your emotions? The next few exercises will help you practice being present to your environment and the sensations in your body, and noticing your judgmental feelings. But it's also okay if you find other interventions in this book more helpful. Everyone's brain is different, so different exercises work better for different people.

Mindful Breathing

As discussed in chapter 4, your breath has a powerful impact on your brain and stress response. Since breathing is something you do mindlessly most of the time, it is a straightforward way to practice mindfulness. Your breath is something that is always happening, so it's always something that you can become present to.

This practice is usually done while sitting in a chair or on a cushion on the floor in a comfortable space where you will not be disturbed.

1. Set a timer for one minute.

2. Sit up straight. Relax your shoulders and face, and guide your attention to your breath.

3. Don't try to control your breath, but just pay attention to the sensations of breathing and the sensations that arise from your body.

4. Allow your eyes to close if it helps you pay closer attention to your breath.

5. If your mind wanders, or you get distracted by feelings or thoughts that spin through your head, that's fine. Just acknowledge the distraction, and guide your attention back to your breath.

Practice this once a day for a week. If you found one minute very easy, and want more of a challenge, then extend the exercise to two or three minutes. If you found this challenging, or weren't sure you were doing it right, not to worry. Wondering whether you are doing it right is very common. When you notice yourself wondering, simply acknowledge that thought and guide your attention back to your breath.

You can also keep this mindful breathing log to encourage your mindful breathing practice. Visit http://www.newharbinger.com/42426 to download this log.

Mindful Breathing Log

Log your practice of mindful breathing. Fill in the date and start time. After completing each practice, enter the duration of the practice session—how long you practiced mindful breathing.

	Day 1	Day 2	Day 3	Day 4	Day 5	Day 6	Day 7
Date							
Start time							
Duration							

There's an App for That

Many people like using a mindfulness app, which guide you through your mindfulness practice. There are many out there to choose from. Headspace focuses on ten-minute meditations and is really easy to use. 10% Happier is also a great way to practice mindfulness. Happy Not Perfect is one that I contributed to and mainly asks you to take a brief mindful moment. Try one out. You may like it.

Alternatively, you can record the steps in the body scan that follows, and then let the recording of your own voice guide you through the steps. If you decide to do this, be sure to speak slowly enough, at a comfortable pace.

Body Scan

One of the simplest mindfulness techniques is a body scan. Your goal is to shift your spotlight of attention to different parts of your body, in turn, and see what you see (or feel what you feel). I've written a specific way to do this exercise, but there's no one right way. Feel free to play around with where you guide your attention. I wrote it to be done sitting in a chair, but you can adapt it to sitting on the floor or lying down.

- Place one hand over your heart, the other on your belly—to remind yourself that you exist in a body. Feel your heart beating. Take a deep breath and exhale. Feel your body expand and contract on the breath—the sensations in your chest and belly.

- Take another deep breath, and on the exhale, let your hands fall into your lap.

- Feel the weight of your hands on your lap and your lap pressing back into your hands.

- Notice the weight of your body on the chair, how the chair feels beneath you. Notice the pressure of the chair against your back.

- As you exhale, notice the tension or relaxation in your shoulders.

- Notice your feet upon the floor. Pay attention to your right foot, then your left foot. How do your toes feel? Your heels?

- Let your awareness drift up to your legs. Can you feel anything there?

- Notice your groin and your buttocks. Any clenching or tingling?

- Then turn your attention to your stomach. Are you clenching or tightening any muscles?

- Notice your hands. Are they clenched or relaxed?

- Then bring your attention upward to your neck, and notice what you feel there.

- Bring your attention to your jaw. Is it tight or loose?

- Bring your attention to your face. What expression are you making?

- Return your attention to your breath. In and out—noticing again the sensation of breathing.

- Take one more deep smooth breath. If the corners of your mouth drift up in a smile, that's okay. Exhale, and go on about your day.

Was there anything particularly difficult about this exercise? What did you notice about your body, and what did you notice about your thoughts?

_____

_____

_____

Daily Opportunities for Mindfulness

You don't have to set aside your regular activities for mindfulness. You can apply it to the things you already have to do.

Think of some activities you have to do, that you don't like doing that much, such as washing dishes, folding laundry, writing, or some task you have to do at work.

Pick a chore from your list above, and be mindful while you are doing it. Don't rush through it. By rushing, you're buying into your own perspective that it's bad, and that bad things need to be avoided. Be deliberate. Pay attention to the physical sensations, the little details.

Often the issue with chores is that we have a thought like *This is boring*. And we (A) automatically assume that's true and (B) automatically assume that boring is bad. Maybe it's not boring, and that thought is just getting in the way of you enjoying it. Or yes, it is boring, but that doesn't mean it's bad—it's just a part of life. If all of life were exciting, then you couldn't really appreciate the excitement.

Mindful Eating

Eating is something you do everyday, and because it is such a common event, it's very easy to do mindlessly. But in this exercise, you're going to be asked to do it mindfully, with intention, paying full attention to the food you are eating, without judgment.

1. Take a raisin or a grape or a slice of orange or a cashew…any small item of food that you can easily fit in your mouth. Don't choose either your favorite food or something you strongly dislike.

2. Hold the food in your hand. Examine it like it's a piece of art, a sculpture. What do you notice about how it looks—the small folds, textures, and shadows? How does it feel in your hand?

3. Place it to your lips. Notice the texture, perhaps the scent wafting to your nose.

4. Place it in your mouth and bite into it. Notice the sensations on your tongue and cheeks, how it feels…the smell again. Has it changed?

5. Chew slowly to unlock the flavor. Notice the flavor, and notice what you notice.

6. Notice perhaps your urge to automatically swallow. Chew one more time than you think is necessary. And then again. Has the flavor changed? Notice whether you are liking it less or more now.

7. Take one more bite, and then swallow intentionally.

Was there anything particularly difficult about this exercise? What did you notice about your body, and what did you notice about your thoughts as you were mindfully eating?

_____

_____

_____

_____

Importantly, this is not the way you should eat all the time. Most of the time, you can enjoy what you're eating and the company you're with. But there are elements of mindfulness that are helpful with any meal, particularly if you take a moment of mindfulness before you start eating.

Challenges With Acceptance

Many people have physical problems in their bodies that exacerbate their depression, augment their anxiety, or get in the way of feeling better. This can include chronic pain, breathing issues, diabetes, irritable bowel syndrome, or any other chronic condition.

When that is the case, the biggest problem is often not so much the body's limitations as it is the brain's overreaction to those limitations. Yes, there may be an issue with the body—something painful. If you can do something to get better, do it. And if you can't do anything, then it's helpful to accept that as a limitation. Taking this step reduces stress, which can even start to benefit your underlying condition, and frees you to focus on what you *can* control.

A Note About Positive Emotions

Often when we are very excited about a positive feeling or something enjoyable, inherent in that excitement is a fear or sadness that it will be over soon. In depression, a positive feeling like this can feel like a life preserver keeping you afloat—but if you treat that feeling like it's the only thing that will prevent you from drowning, then you're likely to have a lot of anxiety about it being taken away. Instead, it's helpful to recognize that while positive feelings support you, they're not essential every moment.

So while positive emotions are enjoyable and helpful, and even necessary in the long term, in the short term, you can still survive and accomplish meaningful things without them. Once you accept that you do not need positive emotions every moment, then you don't have to worry as much about whether they will always be there or not, and you can appreciate them for what they are.

Conclusion

Shakespeare's Hamlet says, "There is nothing either good or bad, but thinking makes it so." Being mindful of your thoughts and your automatic judgments is a powerful tool. But like any useful tool, it's not right for everything. It won't fix every problem.

Sometimes mindlessness is useful too—getting lost in enjoyment or distraction. Let your mind wander.

If you're feeling unhappy or anxious, or any other negative emotion, it's perfectly fine to distract yourself from it. Focus on something else. Entertain yourself. Watch TV. Play a game. There is nothing wrong with distraction. Or better yet, try to fix the problem. That's a great path forward too. Some problems are easily fixed. Others are easily forgotten once you take your mind off them.

The only problem with mindlessness is if it's your only response to negative feelings—this may allow you to feel better in the moment, but you end up not actually experiencing your life.

However, since so many of us are mindless so much of the time, being mindful is a skill worth developing. It helps you to get in touch with your emotions and yet not be a slave to them. It helps with accepting the things you can't change, allowing you to focus on the things that you can. And it can be particularly important in changing habits, which comes next.

Chapter 9

The Habit Spiral

Over 100 years ago, the autopilot feature on airplanes was developed so that a plane could make progress toward its destination without constant attention and intervention by the pilot. It was originally very crude, but autopilot has greatly improved as airplane technology has advanced. By contrast, this feature of the brain developed over a hundred million years ago, and it hasn't really changed all that much. This is the habit system of the brain.

The habit system refers primarily to a deep region of the brain called the striatum. The striatum is very strongly connected to the amygdala, and thus habits, emotions, and stress are inextricably linked. Stress triggers us to enact our habits, particularly our most deeply ingrained habits. And acting out those habits reduces stress, at least in the short term. When those habits are also beneficial in the long term, we call them good habits. If not, we call them bad habits. But the striatum does not make a distinction.

In F. Scott Fitzgerald's novel *This Side of Paradise*, the struggling romantic main character declares, "I'm a slave to my emotions, to my likes, to my hatred of boredom, to most of my desires." Perhaps you can identify with this, and it's actually part of the reason you feel stuck.

Not following your habits and instead forging a new path can be very scary. Changing the status quo gets the limbic system all fired up and activates the stress response. To calm itself, that limbic activation triggers the striatum to compel you back to your old habits. Trying to deviate from your routine triggers your habits even more strongly. The good news is that you can retrain your striatum with more helpful habits.

When it comes to happiness and overcoming depression, there is nothing wrong with having habits. It's a problem only if you have the sense that you're not really living your life, that it's being lived for you by some programmed routine. Luckily, while you are the computer program (the striatum), you are also the programmer (the prefrontal cortex). You can't rewrite the whole code, but you can tinker with it and work out a few of the bugs.

This chapter focuses on how to take advantage of the habit circuitry in the brain so that your life starts falling into place without so much conscious, willful effort. This chapter explores the neuroscience of habit formation and habit change. It builds on previous chapters to help you identify unhelpful habits and learn how best to create more helpful ones.

Identifying Unhelpful Habits

You can have coping habits in all sorts of domains. The most obvious are behavioral habits, regular actions that you take, like checking your email, drinking a beer, procrastinating, and more. But you can also have social habits and emotional habits, and even thinking habits. In depression, all these different types of habits tend to reinforce each other to keep you stuck.

One of the best first steps to creating an upward spiral is to become aware of the ways that you're unintentionally creating a downward spiral. It can be appealing to ignore negative habits, berate yourself for creating them in the first place, or resign yourself to them. But those automatic judgments, criticisms, and feelings of despair are all simply habits themselves—cognitive and emotional ones—that contribute to your depression. That's why mindfulness can be so powerful in changing habits. The first step isn't to change anything but to just become more aware of what's going on.

In fact, even when you identify unhelpful habits, the goal is not to change them—instead, you need to replace them with new helpful habits. As Timothy Gallwey describes beautifully in one of my favorite books on mindfulness, *The Inner Game of Tennis*, "A child doesn't have to break the habit of crawling… He simply leaves it as he finds walking an easier way to get around" (Gallwey, 1997, p. 67).

Look at the list of coping habits on the next page, and put a check next to any that you have done several times over the past few months. Don't worry about whether they're good or bad, because the striatum doesn't.

- ☐ Socializing
- ☐ Isolating yourself
- ☐ Procrastinating or ignoring
- ☐ Worrying
- ☐ Exercising
- ☐ Eating
- ☐ Cooking/baking
- ☐ Drinking alcohol
- ☐ Drinking caffeinated beverages
- ☐ Avoiding difficulty
- ☐ Getting angry or aggressive
- ☐ Blaming yourself
- ☐ Taking drugs
- ☐ Deep breathing
- ☐ Planning
- ☐ Organizing
- ☐ Taking a shower/bath
- ☐ Doing chores

- ☐ Ruminating or wallowing
- ☐ Writing creatively
- ☐ Writing a letter or email
- ☐ Avoiding emails
- ☐ Drawing
- ☐ Playing or listening to music
- ☐ Playing a game
- ☐ Doing a crossword or puzzle
- ☐ Shopping
- ☐ Getting takeout
- ☐ Reading
- ☐ Meditating
- ☐ Dancing
- ☐ Yelling
- ☐ Driving
- ☐ Praying
- ☐ Stretching or doing yoga

This list is merely a sampling of the many habits people use to cope. The list could go on and on. It's helpful to think of these habits as tools: they're neither good nor bad in themselves; they just serve different purposes. For example, a hammer and a screwdriver are both tools, but is one a better tool than the other? It depends on what you're working on, doesn't it?

It's all about choice. Choice means that if you don't like your habits, you can change them—and that if you don't like what your habits are compelling you to do, you don't have to do it.

If you don't feel like you're in charge of your own autopilot, then you're going to encounter some problems. Just like on an airplane, running on autopilot isn't for every situation. The pilot has to set the destination and land the plane. Yes, autopilot is very helpful in doing most of the work, but there are some critical things that autopilot can't do. The same is true of the brain.

The striatum is very powerful and will help you accomplish a lot. But it can't do everything. The prefrontal cortex has to set the destination. For the most part, you can, and should, let the striatum run on autopilot. But if you change the destination or need to be flexible, then the prefrontal cortex has to intervene.

Happiness is best achieved when the habits in the striatum and the goals directed by the prefrontal cortex are aligned. But if you want your habits to become more aligned with your goals, you will need to retrain your striatum to do something different, and that takes some effort.

Journaling Your Events and Habits

Keep a journal to identify some emotional, thinking, and behavioral habits. Over the next week, write down events, situations, or interactions that led you to feel bad. Clarify the feelings, thoughts, and behaviors that came next, and where that led you. The goal of this is simply awareness. You don't need to try to change anything; the idea is to become more aware of your tendencies. You can write in your own journal or write in the space provided here. If you need more space, visit http://www.newharbinger.com/42426 to download this journal.

Journal of Events and Habits

What happened?	How did you feel at the time?	What did you think at the time?	What did you do?	How did you feel afterward?
Example: *My boss criticized my performance at work.*	*Attacked and underappreciated*	*I'm bad at my job and I can't do anything right.*	*Sat on my couch and ate ice cream.*	*Weak, and pathetic*
1.				
2.				
3.				
4.				

What happened?	How did you feel at the time?	What did you think at the time?	What did you do?	How did you feel afterward?
5.				
6.				
7.				
8.				

Looking at your journal, can you identify some problematic patterns? What about if you think about the last few months or years: what are some unhelpful behavioral habits that you engage in?

_____

_____

_____

_____

Unhelpful thought patterns, like black-or-white thinking and catastrophizing, can also be thought of as habits. Can you think of any unhelpful emotional or thinking habits that you engage in?

_____

_____

_____

_____

What are some unhelpful social habits that you engage in?

_____

_____

_____

_____

Creating New Habits

In his classic and best-selling book, _How to Win Friends and Influence People_, Dale Carnegie (2010) writes about fishing in Maine: "Personally I am very fond of strawberries and cream, but I have found that for some strange reason, fish prefer worms. So when I went fishing, I didn't think about what I wanted. I didn't bait the hook with strawberries and cream. I dangled a worm" (p. 30). If you want to change the striatum, you've got to start speaking its language. Yes, *you* care strongly about whether you've got good or bad habits, but the striatum doesn't.

The striatum doesn't always have to work against you. It can work for you, but like a dog, it has to be trained. Training is about consistency. If your dog jumps on the couch, and sometimes you yell at him to get off, and others times you plop down and cuddle with him, then he will be very confused about what you want from him.

Consistency does not require you to be a jerk. You wouldn't hit your dog for making a mistake, and likewise, it doesn't help to berate yourself. If it takes your dog a little longer to learn, then you just need to be more patient. The same goes for you.

Self-criticism is one means of activating the prefrontal cortex to try to regulate the limbic system, and it's linked to activation of the anterior cingulate—the mistake region of the brain (Longe et al., 2010). But this pattern of thinking can get in the way of making positive change, particularly if you're feeling down and demotivated. By contrast, self-reassurance uses the parts of the PFC that more directly regulate the emotional limbic system. It also activates the insula, the part of the brain that feels things and is linked to empathy. Self-reassurance therefore helps with making positive changes. So you can either feel your emotions empathically and start to make a change or, through old coping habits, avoid feeling them and stay on the same course. The choice is up to you.

Creating new habits is hard. Fortunately, the more you repeat an action, the more strongly it gets encoded in the dorsal striatum, and the easier it becomes. The first few times, trying a new habit often feels awkward and uncomfortable. It requires a lot of willpower from the prefrontal cortex. Over time, it starts to feel more natural as it gets encoded into the striatum. But it requires time—and repetition—just like training a dog.

Use Self-Affirmation

When it comes to habits, most of us think about what we don't like about ourselves, and heap on self-criticism. Thus, trying to change habits can be quite stressful, which itself triggers habits and makes it harder to change. And there's a better way.

Research has shown that habits can be easier to change if you focus not on your worst qualities but on your best ones (Epton, Harris, Kane, van Koningsbruggen, & Sheeran, 2015). Think about what you like most about yourself: what qualities of yours would you not want to change? This type of focus is rewarding and activates the nucleus accumbens (Dutcher et al., 2016).

Giving Self-Affirmation

Think back over the past few years of your life, and consider the following questions. If you answer yes, then put a check mark next to the question, and describe your answer in a bit more detail.

1. Have you done something nice for someone else that you didn't have to do? ☐

     _____

     _____

2. Have you forgiven someone who hurt you? ☐

     _____

     _____

3. When making a decision, have you taken someone else's feelings into consideration? ☐

     _____

     _____

4. Have you helped out someone less fortunate than you? ☐

     _____

     _____

5. Have you provided help or support to a friend or family member? ☐

     _____

     _____

Recognize the Triggers

All habits are triggered by something. Unfortunately, for many bad habits, the trigger is a feeling like anxiety or disappointment. Fortunately, you've been working throughout this book to help reduce those feelings. Anything you do to alleviate stress will help reduce the pull of bad habits.

And, regardless of what the trigger is, by recognizing the trigger to an unhelpful habit, you can put a plan in place before it happens. You can visualize ahead of time how you would rather respond to the trigger instead of following your bad habit. That helps the prefrontal cortex override the stimulus-response nature of the striatum. Since unhelpful habits often trigger further unhelpful habits, a little bit of planning can help break the cycle and prevent a downward spiral.

And for some straightforward bad habits that are triggered by an event or an object, there's an even simpler solution: eliminate the trigger. Let's say you're trying to be productive while working from home, but you always end up watching TV. You could try to use more willpower to resist watching TV, or you could just go somewhere without a TV. It's much easier to avoid temptation than to resist it.

Recognizing Your Triggers

Answer the following questions to figure out what your biggest triggers are. Your journal of events and habits may help provide some insight.

1. What thoughts often precede your negative feelings?

   _____

   _____

   _____

2. What types of interactions make you feel worse or trigger bad habits?

   _____

   _____

   _____

3.   What environments or situations make you feel worse or trigger bad habits?

_____

_____

_____

Now that you know what your triggers are, you can plan how to respond with better coping habits in the future. The next exercise is kind of like a Mad Libs word game. Use it to plan how you'll respond the next time you're triggered.

Coping Habits Word Game

When _____ (event or sensation) makes me feel like, or

think about doing, _____ (unhelpful habit), I will accept

those thoughts and feelings, and then I will _____ (helpful habit).

Change Your Environment

The ultimate trigger is the environment around you. This provides the context to your life. Your hippocampus understands your context implicitly and feeds this information to the striatum.

Are you at work? You'll feel compelled to act one way. Are you at grandma's house? A party? The type of environment you're in dictates the type of habits you're likely to engage in.

Again, changing your environment is one way to affect your habits. This is why recovering alcoholics are advised to stay away from bars and not hang out with the people they used to drink with. Yes, you can override habits, but why make it difficult on yourself?

Are you having difficulty being productive at home? You don't need to always be mindful of your thoughts or try to decrease your stress. Just leave your house. Don't feel like exercising at home? No problem. Just get dressed in workout clothes and drive to the gym. Simply by moving to a new environment that's more conducive to whatever new habit you're trying to create, you're likely to feel more motivated to do it.

Good Habits Can Trigger More Good Habits

Here are some necessary actions that help you feel better about yourself and also change your environment. The hippocampus recognizes the changed context and essentially says, "Oh, I guess we care about ourselves."

- Get dressed

- Make your bed

- Brush your teeth

- Take a shower

- Do your laundry

- Exercise

- Call a friend

Reward Yourself

When you're training a dog to sit when you say the command, then every time he does it correctly, you should give him a treat. That's how you train a dog. If you want to train new habits, then reward yourself.

How Will You Reward Yourself?

Here are some ideas for how to reward yourself. Add others that appeal to you, and put a check next to the ones that you will use.

- ☐ Tell yourself you did a good job.

- ☐ Treat yourself to a small snack.

- ☐ Relax for fifteen minutes.

- ☐ Give yourself a checkmark or a gold star.

☐ Eat a piece of candy.

☐ Take a deep breath.

☐ Smile.

☐ Call a friend and tell them what you did.

☐ _____

☐ _____

How You Benefit from Bad Habits

It's important to acknowledge how you benefit from bad habits. We all have bad habits for a reason. We have them because they help us, or at least they helped us in the past when we first developed them.

Understanding how we benefit from habits can lead to some important insights. For one, it can help grant you some acceptance: to see that you're not crazy, that you're doing things for a reason. Second, it can create a path forward, by seeing what you need in your life and perhaps finding a more constructive way of getting it.

Our habits reduce uncertainty and create a greater sense of perceived control, both of which help to reduce stress. For example, if you are worried about awkward social interactions, you may tend to avoid all social interactions. That can lower stress in the short-term, but is not a good long-term solution (see chapter 6). Because bad habits—even destructive habits—are so familiar, we find momentary comfort in them. But that comfort is gained at the expense of long-term well-being.

Some habits can create brief positive feelings—like wasting time on the Internet, eating unhealthy food, or smoking—because they provide a brief burst of dopamine, which momentarily helps us feel better. Unfortunately, it's a fleeting feeling that ultimately leads to more negative emotions.

Don't think that you need to eliminate all your bad habits—they can be a great source of stress relief—but at least create some good habits to counteract the negative effects. On the other hand, if your habits are getting in the way of living your life, then changing them will have a powerfully positive impact on your mood, anxiety, and life satisfaction.

In what ways do your bad habits benefit you?

_____

_____

_____

_____

_____

Can you think of more helpful ways to get these same benefits?

_____

_____

_____

_____

_____

Facing Your Fears

At heart, unhelpful habits are about avoidance. We don't like how we feel, so we try to avoid feeling it, or take action to change the way we feel. But while that calms us down momentarily, it trains the striatum that this feeling is, in fact, something to be avoided. And the more we avoid it, the more we feel compelled to avoid it in the future. This process of following the path of least resistance just succeeds in making all your fears and anxieties seem bigger and bigger.

The only way to eliminate fear and anxiety is to teach your brain that they are not something to be afraid of. Choose to move toward the fear. You don't have to do it, but insofar as the fear is getting in the way of things that are important to you, then it's something you actually *want* to do.

This is a form of one of the most powerful treatments for anxieties: exposure therapy. You can try facing your fears on your own, or find a mental health professional to guide you in the process.

That Little Voice in Your Head

There's a little voice in your head that tells you to give up. It tells you to turn on the TV and eat junk food. It tells you you're worthless, and that everything is pointless. It becomes the running commentary on your life—as if your subconscious were live-tweeting everything you do. It is distracting and depressing, and at times overwhelming. But it is part of your habit system, and you have the power to lessen its grip over you.

Whenever the voice whispers something, and you do it, then you make it stronger and harder to ignore. This is just how the dorsal striatum works. The thought is the trigger, and by believing it and acting on it, you're rewarding it. That just makes it more likely to happen the next time. If every time your dog barked, you gave it a treat, it would start to bark a lot more.

But each time you ignore the voice, it gets potentially easier to ignore the next time. Now, this is not a linear progression. There will be times when you're more confident and energetic, and the voice will be easy to ignore. And there will be times when you're down or upset or empty, and the voice will seem like everything. But each time you summon the will to ignore it, and do something else, the more you will foster a new cognitive habit.

Imagine you've planted a new lawn. Staying off that lawn for a few days will help it grow. If you forget and walk across it, you won't destroy all your hard work, so there's no need to be despondent. All you can do is remember to avoid the lawn the next time. If you remember more than you forget, then you're coming out ahead.

When you're trying to change your habits, or do something uncomfortable, what does that little voice in your head tell you?

_____

_____

_____

_____

_____

Now that you know what your voice is telling you, can you spot any trends? Do you notice any cognitive distortions in what it's saying? How might you respond?

_____

_____

_____

_____

_____

_____

Eating Habits

While there's not enough time to explore all kinds of habits, I'll go a bit more in depth on one in particular: eating. Eating habits have a big effect on your well-being and are illustrative of all habits in general.

Eating isn't just about survival. It's also about feelings and culture and connection with others. That includes not just what you eat but also how and why you eat, which can all impact your well-being.

Many studies have shown over the years that people with depression tend to eat an unhealthier diet. But what hasn't been clear until recently is that there's a causal relationship. So does depression contribute to unhealthy eating, or does unhealthy eating contribute to depression? As with most things in this book, the answer is a bit of both. But before getting to what you should be eating, I want to discuss how you should be eating and why.

How You Eat

How you eat can have a greater impact on your mood than what you eat. For example, are you eating mindlessly while watching TV? It's better to pay attention to what you put in your mouth. Ideally, you will enjoy it and savor it, but even the simple act of paying attention is beneficial. Being fully present while eating not only decreases stress but can decrease depressive symptoms and make food more enjoyable and satisfying (Winkens et al., 2018).

In addition, eating alone can increase risk for depression (Kurodo et al., 2015). Have more of your meals with other people to take advantage of the social spiral.

Why You Eat

Do you use food to help you deal with your feelings? Eating can be a powerful coping habit. Comfort food is comforting because it releases dopamine and even oxytocin, which leads to a decrease in stress hormones. But when eating habits become a problem, it's important to recognize why you're eating. Are you eating because you're hungry or because you're bored or stressed or uncomfortable in some other way? It's very important to remember that your desire to eat is very different from hunger.

You might feel compelled to eat, but does that mean you're hungry? And even if you are hungry, does that mean you need to eat? No, you're not going to starve.

Most people, at some point, use food as a coping mechanism to deal with their feelings. There's nothing wrong with doing that occasionally. It can be a fun and delicious coping habit. But if it starts to be a problem, then it creates the potential for a downward spiral.

The issue is that the reason we have an urge to eat has to do with a feeling, and food is not a replacement for feelings. One of my favorite quotes from a scientific article comes from a study on morbid obesity. The authors of the study point out how it's not about the weight or the food but about what the weight and the food mean—what they represent. The authors write that the mental and emotional benefits of food are "profound, though not curative" and that "it's hard to get enough of something that *almost* works" (Felitti, Jakstis, Pepper, & Ray, 2010, p. 28). Eating to deal with your feelings won't work in the long term, because the food is not really the thing you're after. Maybe you can get enough comfort for the moment, but the craving will come back, because you can never really get enough of something that's almost the right thing.

The food writer Michael Pollan likes to say, "If you're not hungry enough to eat an apple, you're not hungry." You might feel the sensations of hunger, but there's some other desire at work. You want enjoyment. You want satisfaction. You want peace of mind. You want to feel different than you do now. While food can sometimes give you those things, you'll have a problem if it's the only way you get them.

What You Eat

One Australian study of thousands of teenagers showed that eating a healthier diet led to better overall mental health; more fresh fruits and vegetables and whole grains meant less depression (Jacka et al., 2011). These foods help your brain function optimally, as they provide the building blocks for the brain's essential chemicals. Fresh fruits and vegetables provide key vitamins and minerals for your brain, and foods like fish and olive oil provide important fats to aid in brain function. For more info, check out http://www.choosemyplate.gov/.

One of the problems with processed foods is that they often contain lots of sugar. Sugar stimulates the reward pathways in the brain like an addictive drug, though to a lesser degree, releasing dopamine in the nucleus accumbens (Rada, Avena, & Hoebel, 2005). That's not necessarily a bad thing, because it can also bring pleasure. But it can become problematic because eating sugar can make you crave sugar even more. Ultimately that can disrupt your enjoyment of more natural foods.

Another way that diet affects mood is by changing the kinds of bacteria you've got growing inside your gut. These trillions of bacterial cells assist your body in digestion and the creation of numerous different chemicals that influence your body and brain. Changing your diet can modify your gut bacteria, which can in turn help your mood (Foster & McVey Neufeld, 2013).

Below is a list of foods to try to eat more of. The purpose of changing your eating habits is not to lose weight but simply to consume more healthy food and less unhealthy food. In one study, people who made these dietary changes had about double the improvement in depressive symptoms compared to a control group (Jacka et al., 2017). These dietary changes aren't necessarily a treatment for depression on their own, but they're part of a balanced approach.

- Whole grains (five to eight servings per day)
- Vegetables (six servings per day)
- Fruit (three servings per day)
- Legumes (three to four servings per day)
- Low-fat and unsweetened dairy foods (two to three servings per day)
- Raw and unsalted nuts (one serving per day)
- Fish (at least two servings per week)
- Lean red meats (three to four servings per week)
- Chicken (two to three servings per week)
- Eggs (up to six servings per week)
- Olive oil (three tablespoons per day)

In addition to the above recommendations, try to reduce your consumption of the following: sweets, refined cereals, fried food, fast foods, processed meats, and sugary drinks (no more than three per week). Hard liquor and beer should be reduced as well. On the other hand, most studies agree that a glass of wine (preferably red) is okay with your meal.

Conclusion

The main problem with your habits is that they're perfectly content to go on living your life without you. They don't care about your happiness or long-term well-being. But *you* probably care about those things. You could ask them nicely to give you your life back, but they'll probably just ignore you.

Importantly, you do not have to convince your habits to let you go. Even if your personal auto-pilot compels you to fly a certain course, you don't have to follow it.

You have the power to choose something else—anything else. But knowing you have this power can actually increase limbic activity, which can feel uncomfortable. The novelist Milan Kundera described this as "the unbearable lightness of being." It's often more comfortable to pretend like you don't have control over your life. But you do.

To start living your life again, you do not have to avoid all habits, but just choose the ones you like, the ones taking you in the direction you want to go. That's not always easy, but if it's important to you, then there is meaning in the struggle.

Creating new habits can be difficult, but think about why they're important to you and how you will benefit. Sometimes all it takes is a deep breath and a calm reminder to yourself that you have the power to choose a new path forward.

Chapter 10

The Gratitude and Compassion Spiral

The Greek stoic philosopher Epictetus once said, "He is a wise man who does not grieve for the things which he has not, but rejoices for those which he has." The ancient Greeks understood that it is not our circumstances that create happiness, but our thinking about our circumstances. That's great news, because, while reality is often hard to change, your perception of reality is much more malleable. It's influenced by what you pay attention to, which in turn impacts your brain activity and chemistry.

In depression, that can work against you as the brain becomes biased to pay more attention to negative information. But fortunately, you can counteract that by guiding your attention to the more positive parts of reality—the people who support you, the things you appreciate. As you pay more attention to the positive aspects of your life, it's easier to experience positive emotions, which helps create an upward spiral out of depression (Sin & Lyubomirsky, 2009; Chaves, Lopez-Gomez, Hervas, & Vazquez, 2017).

Sometimes it's hard to appreciate the good things we have, because they're not as good as we might have hoped. That's particularly true when it comes to appreciating your own good qualities. Thus, in order to appreciate the things you have, it's helpful to be forgiving and compassionate.

This chapter will help guide your focus to the parts of your life to be grateful for that your brain may be overlooking or distorting. Part of that journey will involve exercises in self-compassion and forgiveness. Importantly, the key to this chapter is not about feeling more grateful, which you don't have control over, but rather about recognizing things to be grateful for. That will make the difference.

The Challenges and Benefits of Gratitude

In depression, the dopamine system isn't quite functioning properly, so it's understandable why you don't think about things to be grateful for: they don't inspire a spark of joy. Maybe you've had well-meaning friends who asked you to snap out of it and focus on all the wonderful parts of your life. Maybe you've even tried but felt an emptiness where you thought you should feel joy. That can make you feel ungrateful, and no one wants to feel ungrateful. Isn't it just easier to forget all about it?

That's why I want to emphasize the fact that I'm not asking you to feel grateful. You cannot control your feelings, but you can control your actions and your focus, at least to some extent. Focus your attention on the positive parts of reality, and forgive yourself for your shortcomings.

Numerous studies have shown the benefits of gratitude. Gratitude can decrease depression symptoms as well as stress in general, and leads to increased perception of social support (Wood, Maltby, Gillett, Linley, & Joseph, 2008). It improves self-esteem and psychological well-being (Lin, 2015). It can even improve your physical health and the quality of your sleep (Hill, Allemand, & Roberts, 2013; Wood, Joseph, Lloyd, & Atkins, 2009).

Gratitude has so many benefits because it affects a wide variety of brain regions and chemicals. Importantly, gratitude has the power to activate the dopamine system, specifically the brain stem region where dopamine is produced (Zahn et al., 2009). This means it can have wide-ranging effects on reward and enjoyment. But rather than list all the rest of the brain benefits of gratitude, I'll let you discover them throughout this chapter.

Gratitude for the Past

The existentialist Albert Camus wrote about an "invincible summer" that exists in all of us—deep positive memories that can carry us through difficult times. Interestingly, sadness can sometimes direct our attention toward these moments that we are grateful for. We can be sad something is over and also grateful that we experienced it in the first place. They are two sides of the same coin. Everything comes to an end. But the fact that something ends is not a reason to eschew gratitude. Things are meaningful *because* they end, and we have them for a time.

Importantly, the brain is complex, and it's possible to feel many emotions at once. You can feel sad and grateful at the same time, as well as angry, relieved, or anxious. But it is not really possible to focus on all of those emotions at the same time, and the ones we focus on have a powerful effect.

Thinking of happy memories activates production of serotonin in the anterior cingulate cortex (Perreau-Linck et al., 2007). It also activates the nucleus accumbens, signifying release of motivating dopamine (Speer, Bhanji, & Delgado, 2014). Modulating key neurotransmitters in key brain regions is a win-win.

Remembering Happy Times

List some happy memories here—not in detail, but just a few words to jog your memory. Remember that time when:

- _____
- _____
- _____
- _____
- _____
- _____
- _____
- _____

Thinking about happy memories can actually improve happiness more than writing about them, since you reexperience them rather than analyze them (Lyubomirsky, Sousa, & Dickerhoof, 2006). So here is a visualization exercise.

Visualize a Happy Time

Pick a moment from the past to think about. You could have been with another person or you might have been alone but somewhere wonderful. Start with some deep, slow breaths (see chapter 3). Then set a timer for one minute and visualize your happy memory in detail. Imagine the colors, the smells, the textures, and the sounds of the place. If you were with someone else, recall how this person looked and what he or she did or said.

At the end of one minute, pay attention to how you feel. If you feel good, then know that this memory is part of your own invincible summer that you can return to when needed.

Gratitude for the Future

Optimism is a form of gratitude—it is being grateful for what the future may hold. Unfortunately, optimism can be stressful, because you don't always have control over how things turn out. That is one reason why most people with depression display pessimism—to protect themselves, their limbic system, and their nucleus accumbens against disappointment. So even though it may be uncomfortable, take a moment to acknowledge what you're hopeful for.

What difficulties are you experiencing right now that have the possibility of getting better in the future?

_____

_____

_____

_____

What potential good things may happen in the future? This includes positive events occurring and feelings improving. Can you be grateful for the possibility even if you can't be certain these things will happen? (The alternative is never having the possibility at all.)

_____

_____

_____

_____

Gratitude for Others

Humans are social animals, and we need each other to survive and thrive. But it is easy to take our relationships with others for granted. Unfortunately, when we take things for granted, it is very difficult to harness the benefits of gratitude.

Think back over the last few years, and the people who helped you along the way. Write down the names of people who helped you achieve important goals, who supported you through a difficult time, or who just made you smile.

_____

_____

_____

_____

Expressing to other people how much you appreciate them can have a positive impact on their lives. But interestingly, it also can have a positive impact on you, your life, and your brain.

Gratitude increases our sense of connection with others. Studies of gratitude have shown that it activates the same medial prefrontal regions that we utilize to understand the perspective of other people and to act compassionately (Fox, Kaplan, Damasio, & Damasio, 2015). Part of the reason gratitude can help you feel more connected to others is that in recognizing what you are grateful for, you must acknowledge what you need. And in acknowledging what you need, you become aware of the needs of others too. In addition, many of the benefits of gratitude for others are mediated by the oxytocin system (vanOyen Witviliet, et al., 2018). This is an upward spiral, as gratitude facilitates connection with others and connection with others facilitates gratitude.

The next gratitude exercise has been shown to have measurable positive impacts on mood that last for several weeks, and these are accompanied by increases in gratitude-related anterior cingulate activity (Kini, Wong, McInnis, Gabana, & Brown, 2016). It even enhances the effectiveness of other treatments for depression (Wong et al., 2018).

Expressing Thanks

Expressing your gratitude toward other people is a particularly effective means of harnessing the benefits of gratitude and changing brain activity. One of the simplest ways of doing this is by writing a letter expressing your gratitude to someone. Even if you don't send it, it can improve your mood.

One study asked participants to write gratitude letters and found that it changed gratitude-related activity in their anterior cingulate cortex even several months later (Kini et al., 2016). The anterior cingulate region generally responds to self-relevant stimuli. Thus, as you practice being grateful, positive aspects of your life suddenly become more relevant to you. You won't have to look for them so hard, because your brain will be automatically looking for you.

Write a Thank-You Letter

Think about someone in your life who did something for you for which you are grateful and whom maybe you feel like you never adequately thanked. Even if you did thank the person, you can do it again. Perhaps this is someone you listed earlier.

Write a thank-you letter expressing your appreciation to that person. Be specific about why you are grateful and how their behavior affected your life. Set a timer for fifteen minutes and just write. Do not worry about perfect grammar or spelling. (Note: you do not have to send this letter.)

_____

_____

_____

_____

_____

_____

_____

_____

_____

_____

_____

_____

_____

_____

_____

_____

_____

_____

_____

For even more benefits, repeat this exercise two more times over the next couple weeks for a different person each time.

Bonus challenge: Set up a time to meet, and deliver the letter personally. Both you and the other person will benefit.

A Regular Gratitude Practice

A daily reminder of things to be grateful for is a way to practice gratitude. One of the simplest ways to accomplish this is with a gratitude journal. Even in people with mental health disorders, gratitude journals have been shown to increase positive emotions, connectedness, optimism, and to reduce anxiety (Kerr, O'Donovan, & Pepping, 2015). In addition, a regular practice of gratitude helps activate the parasympathetic nervous system and increase heart rate variability, helping you stay calm (Redwine et al., 2016).

Practicing gratitude helps you focus on the wonderful things you get and thus makes it easier to enjoy giving. One study found that gratitude is related to generosity, corresponding to activity in the nucleus accumbens and the motivational parts of the prefrontal cortex (Karns, Moore, & Mayr, 2017). So gratitude allows us to enjoy giving and to be motivated more by the needs of others than our own. Furthermore, with a continued practice of gratitude, the same study found even greater increases in prefrontal activity. Gratitude motivates the desire to help others, and it's something your brain gets better at with practice.

Keep a gratitude journal over the next seven days. Visit http://www.newharbinger.com/42426 to download this gratitude journal for future use.

Gratitude Journal

Keeping in mind that there are many things in life to be grateful for—some big, some small—each day before you go to bed, think back over the past twenty-four hours, and find five things in your life for which you are grateful. Record the date in this journal and write down the five things. These can be specific events that happened over the past day, positive actions you took, or other things that are in your life.

Date	Things to Be Grateful For
1.	1. 2. 3. 4. 5.
2.	1. 2. 3. 4. 5.
3.	1. 2. 3. 4. 5.

4.	1. 2. 3. 4. 5.
5.	1. 2. 3. 4. 5.
6.	1. 2. 3. 4. 5.
7.	1. 2. 3. 4. 5.

While positive events in your life make it easier to feel grateful, they aren't necessary requirements for gratitude. One study found that higher levels of gratitude predicted improvements in depression at three months and at six months. For the three- month time period, these effects were mediated by an increase in positive life events, but that wasn't true at six months. That means that in the short term, gratitude combined with positive life events will help you get better, but in the long term, all that's needed is gratitude—you don't actually need positive life events. Once gratitude becomes a habit, it helps you all on its own (Disabato, Kashdan, Short, & Jarden, 2017).

Bonus challenge: At the end of the week, look over your gratitude journal or just think back to the people who have supported you in big or small ways over the past week. Pick at least one person and send a brief thank-you email, text message, or note. Alternatively, you could make a phone call or say thanks in person. It doesn't have to be long. Even just "Thanks for the support this week" is fine. Repeat each week to see an even greater benefit.

Gratitude for Activities

Chapter 2 recommended doing activities that you enjoy. While these activities are inherently rewarding, you can also use them as an opportunity to practice gratitude. Attention to the positive aspects of your activities, the things you enjoy the most, can enhance your experience of them. For example, attention modulates the brain's motivational and emotional response to food (Siep et al., 2009). It's hard to fully enjoy what you're doing when your mind is somewhere else, so focus your attention on the joy of the present moment. Enjoy the company you're with. Savor the food you're eating.

Here are some moments to savor:

☐ Eating ice cream (or other favorite food)

☐ Going for a walk at sunset

☐ Reading a book

☐ Taking a deep breath

☐ Hanging out with friends

☐ Working up a sweat

These are some suggestions. Feel free to use them or come up with your own moments to savor. Then write about them in your gratitude journal.

Savor the Positive Aspects of Chores

You can utilize gratitude even while doing chores or other mundane tasks. For example, with folding laundry, notice the pleasant smell of freshly laundered socks and the enjoyable symmetry of neatly folded clothes. If you're doing the dishes, enjoy the warm sudsy water.

The next time you are doing a chore, concentrate on its positive aspects. Intentionally immerse yourself in the small joys of the moment. After taking in the pleasant parts of this chore, do you feel differently? Write down anything you notice.

_____

_____

_____

_____

_____

_____

_____

When doing chores, savor the process of putting your life in order in small and necessary ways.

Gratitude for Yourself

In depression, it can feel like you're a big pile of regrets and anxieties. But there's more to you than just the negative aspects that depression directs your attention to. Even if you aren't exactly the person you want to be, it's good to think about the parts of yourself that you're glad are there.

This is a key component of the power of gratitude. Gratitude protects against depression and anxiety not only because it helps your relationships with others but also because it improves your relationship with yourself (Petrocchi & Couyoumdjian, 2016).

What qualities do you appreciate about yourself and would not want to change?

_____

_____

_____

_____

Have you experienced any difficult events that ultimately led to something positive? If so, describe them. This could be a breakup that led to a better understanding of yourself, or it could be losing a job, which led to some positive life change. Even if the positive doesn't make up for the negative, it's helpful to focus on what you got rather than what you lost.

_____

_____

_____

_____

Sometimes it is difficult to appreciate ourselves, because we have qualities that we dislike and cannot overlook. This is where self-compassion comes in.

Compassion and Forgiveness

You don't have to like everything about yourself or a situation or another person to appreciate the positive. Even if your glass of water is 90 percent empty, you can still be grateful for that last little sip. Does that mean you need to ignore the rest of the water that you would like to have but don't? No.

Unfortunately, unless you forgive what's lacking in a situation or a person, then your attention will keep getting drawn back to it. That's particularly true when it comes to yourself, as we often treat ourselves more harshly than we would anyone else. Thus, self-compassion and forgiveness are both helpful in creating an upward spiral (Muris & Petrocchi, 2017).

Self-Compassion Exercise

If you had a friend who was struggling with depression or anxiety, what would you say to provide comfort and to support your friend through it?

_____

_____

_____

_____

_____

_____

_____

Now read what you just wrote, but direct it toward yourself. You have a relationship with yourself, just like you have a relationship with other people. And the same basic brain circuits are involved. Improve your relationship with yourself by being more compassionate and supportive of yourself.

Forgiving Yourself

When you're suffering from depression, the most important place to direct forgiveness is toward yourself. Accept the things you can't change, like your genetics and childhood experiences. This is particularly important if your depression or anxiety or other health condition is getting in the way of fully living your life. Forgiving yourself will allow you to shift your focus from what you can't do to what you *can* do.

Only do this next advanced exercise in self-forgiveness if you're feeling up to it.

Write a Letter to Yourself

Think about your limitations: perhaps the ways in which you compare yourself to others and come up short…or perhaps aspects of yourself that you are embarrassed or ashamed about…or actions you've taken that you feel guilty about. Write a letter to yourself, forgiving yourself for your limitations and perceived shortcomings.

_____

_____

_____

_____

_____

_____

_____

_____

_____

_____

_____

_____

_____

_____

Have you hurt anyone and feel sorry about it? Can you find the strength to apologize to them?

_____

_____

_____

_____

_____

Keep in mind that an apology is a personal acknowledgment that you regret your behavior. The other person is under no obligation to forgive you. That choice is up to them.

Dealing With Being Hurt

While other people have the power to help us, they also have the power to hurt us, intentionally or unintentionally. When someone hurts you, the desire for revenge is visceral and impulsive. Unsurprisingly, it involves the insula and striatum (Billingsley & Losin, 2017). But whether or not the other person is worthy of forgiveness, carrying that hurt around can be devastating for you. In the end, you don't have to decide whether the other person is worthy of forgiveness but, rather, whether forgiveness would help you move forward.

Forgiveness does not mean you have to like or be friends with the other person. Forgiveness is an act of acceptance and actually changes the communication between the prefrontal cortex and the limbic system (Fatfouta, Meshi, Merkl, & Heekeren, 2018). By letting go of your anger and pain, forgiveness can help reduce depression and anxiety (Reed & Enright, 2006). Forgiveness is a power you have, and you are the only one who can choose whether to wield it.

This next exercise facilitates forgiveness and is adapted from a clever study conducted by McCullough, Root, and Cohen (2006). Rather than think about how someone hurt you—or how painful the experience was—you will focus on any resulting positive consequences, even if they were unintentional or unexpected.

Looking at the Bright Side

Set a timer for twenty minutes and write about how someone hurt you, but concentrate on the positive consequences. Perhaps you became stronger as result of this experience, or discovered strengths you didn't know you had. Perhaps you became wiser, more confident, more compassionate. Perhaps you found support in strengthening positive relationships or found release in ending toxic ones. In what ways are you better off or a better person for it? Are there any benefits that might come in the future? Write candidly and honestly. It's okay to express anger, sadness, or any other negative emotions, but guide your attention to the positive, remember to breathe, and focus on letting go. Unlike with gratitude, it would not be helpful to say these things to the other person. This is for your benefit only.

_____

_____

_____

_____

_____

_____

_____

_____

_____

_____

_____

_____

A Rainbow of Positive Emotions

Happiness is layered and complex, like a fine wine. There are so many ways to experience positive emotions. We've already covered some like pleasure, meaningfulness, and connection, but here are a few you might not have thought of that can have a profoundly positive impact on your life.

Awe and Wonder

Picture yourself standing on the shore of the ocean, watching the waves roll in from unknown places beyond the horizon. Imagine staring up at the night sky—the multitude of stars in the darkness, floating like a blanket, making you feel at once both emboldened and insignificant. Visualize yourself high in the mountains—snowcapped peaks receding into the distance, the sky spreading out before you, with a river raging far below.

These types of scenes tend to elicit feelings of awe and can have a powerful impact on your mood. Awe brings you fully into the present moment and increases your sense of well-being (Rudd, Vohs, & Aaker, 2012). It improves mood and provides a greater sense of connectedness (Joye & Bolderdijk, 2015). It can even help us better cope with loss (Koh, Tong, & Yuen, 2017).

Awe is powerful because by tapping into something beyond the self it reduces a focus on yourself. This results in decreased activity in self-focused regions of the prefrontal cortex (Ishizu & Zeki, 2014). The connection to something larger than the self adds meaning to life and can even be spiritual. In fact, many interventions that target spirituality help with stress and depression, even addictions (Gonçalves, Lucchetti, Menezes, & Vallada, 2015).

Awe is an interesting emotion because it is not entirely positive. It can be enjoyable, uncomfortable, overwhelming, or even all of those. While most strong emotions activate the fight-or-flight sympathetic nervous system, awe simultaneously activates the calming rest-and-digest parasympathetic nervous system (Chirico et al., 2017). But it also quickens your breath (Shiota, Neufeld, Yeung, Moser, & Perea, 2011). And sometimes it can be tinged with fear (Stellar et al., 2017). It is both energizing and calming at the same time.

Unfortunately, in depression, it is all too easy to interpret any strong emotion as bad. But try to sit there with it and enjoy it for what it is. Strong emotions are generally not simple, but that adds to the spice of life.

Here are some suggestions for adding more awe and wonder to your life:

☐ Watch a sunset.

☐ Look at the night sky.

☐ Watch a slideshow of awe-inspiring images online.

☐ Stand by the ocean.

☐ Visit a national park.

☐ Put up pictures of awe-inspiring natural scenes in your home or work area.

☐ Stay in a hotel with a view

☐ Hike or drive to a scenic point.

☐ Go to a church, temple, or other religious institution.

☐ Admire the architecture of grand buildings.

☐ Visit an art gallery or sculpture garden.

Immerse Yourself in Nature

Awe is most commonly experienced in nature—the grandeur of Yosemite Valley, the desolate beauty of the desert. In fact, simply being in nature can lower your stress levels and trigger good feelings. One large analysis of many studies found that exposure to nature led to a strong increase of positive emotions as well as a slight decrease in negative emotions (McMahan & Estes, 2015). Nature also helps us feel more connected to other people and the world around us (Joye & Bolderdijk, 2015).

Nature can be combined with many of the other suggestions in this book, such as savoring, mindfulness, or exercise. For example, one study found that a walk in nature has a greater impact on positive emotions than a walk in an urban environment (Berman et al., 2012).

The effects of nature on positive emotions, motivation, and well-being are not necessarily related to your initial sense of connection to nature—that is, you don't have to be a nature lover to experience the benefits (Passmore & Howell, 2014). You also don't have to hike the Appalachian Trail, though feel free to. Small ways of experiencing nature can be beneficial. What are some ways that you can experience nature more? On the list below, check off ways to experience nature that you can do. Feel free to add your own ideas.

☐ Sitting in your backyard

☐ Going to a park

☐ Camping

- ☐ Being surrounded by trees

- ☐ Sitting out in the sunlight

- ☐ Going to a golf course

- ☐ Hiking

- ☐ Sitting by a lake

- ☐ Backpacking

- ☐ Rock climbing (on real rocks)

- ☐ Downhill skiing

- ☐ Cross-country skiing

- ☐ Snowshoeing

- ☐ Having a picnic outdoors

- ☐ _____

- ☐ _____

After choosing some of these to do, mark your activity-scheduling calendar from chapter 2 or your own calendar, and do them!

Relying on Humor

In college, I auditioned for the improv comedy group, but got rejected—on two separate occasions. Not the usual path to neuroscience, but we all have our own journeys. At the suggestion of a friend of a friend, I started doing stand-up comedy instead. That friend of a friend, who later became a late-night comedy writer, taught me one of stand-up comedy's secrets: when you think of something funny, write it down.

Even if you don't think of yourself as a funny person, you probably think of at least one funny thing a day—even if it's only funny to you. Most people don't pay attention to those things. They just let them float out of their heads as quickly as they flew in. But if you pay more attention to those funny things, you can actually cultivate a greater experience of humor (Wellenzohn, Proyer, & Ruch, 2016). On top of that, simply bringing more humor into your life can decrease depressive symptoms and increase happiness, and these effects can last for months.

Humor is rewarding and enjoyable, and thus activates the dopamine-rich nucleus accumbens along with the brain stem region that produces dopamine (Mobbs, Greicius, Abdel-Azim, Menon, & Reiss, 2003). In addition, humor activates motivational parts of the prefrontal cortex, as well as the amygdala (Bartolo, Benuzzi, Nocetti, Baraldi, & Nichelli, 2006). This helps to maintain the important balance between the prefrontal cortex and limbic system that is so essential to long-term well-being. Here are two exercises to take advantage of the brain benefits of humor.

Humor Part 1

Carry around a notebook for one week (or you can use your smartphone), and when something funny happens, write it down. This could be a funny event, conversation, observation, or something clever that just pops into your head.

Bonus exercise: Turn those funny thoughts into full-fledged jokes and perform at an open mic night.

Humor Part 2

Add more humor in your life. Here are some suggestions.

- ☐ Watch a funny TV show

- ☐ Go to a comedy show

- ☐ Watch funny videos online

- ☐ Read comics

- ☐ Watch funny movies

- ☐ Tell jokes or listen to jokes

What or who do you find funny? How can you make that or them a bigger part of your life?

_____

_____

_____

_____

Conclusion

Humor, awe, gratitude, and compassion are all great ways to start an upward spiral, though that doesn't mean they will always be easy. In particular, gratitude can be tough, because to feel gratitude, we have to acknowledge that something fills a desire or a need. Thus, feeling grateful automatically exposes our vulnerability.

But acceptance of this vulnerability is essential to happiness. It is simply a fact of life, and if you don't accept it, then you will continually be distracted by it. This aspect of gratitude shows why it is inextricably linked with empathy and our experience of others. In recognizing our own needs and wants, we automatically connect to the needs and desires of others.

Guide your focus to what you are grateful for. And if you don't feel grateful, please forgive yourself and treat yourself with compassion. It can be hard to let go of a focus on the negative, but doing that is often the best way forward.

Whether large or small, there are so many wonderful gifts that have been bestowed on you by your own hard work or by random luck or other people or the universe. Use these gifts to sustain you, and put them into practice for something greater than yourself. As your upward spiral continues, you can give it a further boost not by being grateful for what you receive but by being grateful for what you can give.

Chapter 11

The Continuing Spiral

After many years of research, I've come to understand that there is no one big solution to depression, but there are many small ones. Simply by making small changes in your thoughts, actions, interactions, and environment, you can change the activity and chemistry of key brain circuits that contribute to depression. Sometimes a small change can have big effects, though the process will not always be straightforward.

It may at times feel like your brain is working against you, but be forgiving—it evolved that way to protect you. When change feels scary it's helpful to keep in mind the words of famed American psychologist Abraham Maslow: "One can choose to go back toward safety or forward toward growth." The traits that can get in your way are also the traits that may benefit you. They are not pieces of garbage to be thrown away, but simply tools that should be put back in the toolbox for another time.

Depression is a terrible condition, making it difficult to do all the things that might help you. Over the course of this book, I've asked a lot of you, and if you do not feel capable, that's okay. I do not mean to imply that the burden is on you to get better. There's a whole field of mental health professionals whose job it is to help you. And they can provide other routes to an upward spiral that you cannot do for yourself.

For many suffering from depression, medication may be a part of their upward spiral. About 40 percent of people with depression get completely better after a few months by simply taking a pill. If you're one of those people, then that's the simplest path forward. The problem is that science does not yet know how to figure out ahead of time if you're one of those people.

There are also neuromodulation treatments, like transcranial magnetic stimulation (TMS) or electroconvulsive therapy (ECT), where neural circuits are directly modulated with magnetic or electric stimulation, respectively. And there are many forms of psychotherapy that have proven effective in treating depression. In fact, this book has taken suggestions from many of them.

Medications, neuromodulation treatments, and even psychotherapy are simply different ways of changing the activity and chemistry of key brain circuits that contribute to depression or anxiety.

All of these treatments work by modulating the brain regions and chemicals that have been high-lighted throughout this book. Different people's brains are just more responsive to one treatment over another, or to various combinations of treatments.

In any case, the actions you take toward helping yourself get better are essential. Professional treatment of depression works better with your involvement. Your doctor is not a sorcerer to cast a spell on you—but a collaborator in your journey to get better. Even in a health care setting, the more involved you are in your treatment, the better off you are (Clever et al., 2006).

If you're dissatisfied with your depression or anxiety, find the phone number of a mental health professional. Get an appointment scheduled. You do not have to take medication or engage in any other treatment that you might not want. If your therapist or physician does not help you feel empowered, then find another. But just remember that you do not have to figure it all out by your-self—there are experts for a reason.

The Journey Continues

You're almost done with this book, but your journey continues. Some days, weeks, or months may be easy, and other times, your depression may threaten to overwhelm you. There is no clear, predictable path out of depression.

But even in depression, it is possible to find meaning. Even in depression, it is possible to find happiness and connection. Even in depression, it is possible to make progress toward valued goals. The depression may go up and down, but that is out of your direct control. Keep on the path you've been going on. Have faith in yourself or in science or in God or in the universe, and keep going.

Take a moment to reflect on the journey you've accomplished so far. Just as with climbing a mountain, it can be tempting to focus solely on the brightly shining peak and how far you have to go until you attain it. And if that's motivating, there's nothing wrong with that. But sometimes it's important to pause and take a breath and look at the dark valley below. Even though you may have further to go, you can still appreciate how far you've come.

As you continue on in the world, remember that you are not broken. You're simply endowed with a human brain, full of miraculous wonders, which unfortunately also creates the potential for sometimes getting stuck in a pattern of depression. When you feel anxiety, that's just the amygdala signaling potential danger. When you feel physical or emotional pain, that's simply the anterior cingulate telling you what it thinks is relevant to your journey. When you get stuck in a worry loop, that's just the prefrontal cortex finding an incomplete solution to solving your anxiety. When you feel defeated, that's just an emotional habit the dorsal striatum has been practicing for years, and that still has the possibility of being retrained.

You can't really blame this cast of characters. They evolved to do these things. You can just hope to live with them and learn better how to provide them with what they need. In depression, like surfing, your goal shouldn't be to avoid the wave, or stop the wave, but simply to ride the wave.

When the road ahead looks too difficult and there doesn't seem to be a way you can go on, that's okay. You don't need to solve all your problems at once. There is always one small step you can take. It doesn't have to be the best decision; it just has to be better than the alternative.

Just take one small step to strengthen your brain, and it will make the next step easier, and the next. Whether that's relying on other people to soothe the brain's emotional circuitry or moving your body to boost serotonin, the opportunity is there to create a new path forward.

Acknowledgments

To harness the power of gratitude, I'd like to express my thanks to the many people who helped me write this book in ways big and small. First, to all the friends with whom I've discussed ideas about the brain or well-being or meaningfulness and more, you may not have realized you were helping me write a book, but thank you nonetheless. Next I'd like to thank my scientific mentors, supporters, and colleagues at UCLA: Mark Cohen, Alexander Bystritsky, Martin Monti, Andy Leuchter, Ian Cook, Michelle Abrams, Bob Bilder, Andrew Fuligni, Wendy Slusser, and Peter Whybrow. Thanks to Elizabeth Hollis Hansen, Vicraj Gill, Brady Kahn, and Jill Marsal for helping this book become a reality. Thanks to my family for their love and encouragement, and particularly to my mother, Regina Pally, for her clinical and neuroscientific expertise. Thanks to Marv Belzer of the UCLA Mindful Awareness Research Center for sharing his passion for, and knowledge of, mindfulness practices. Thanks also to Aimee Hunter, Dara Gharameni, and Joey Cooper for their invaluable input and edits. Thanks to Bruin Ladies Ultimate for inspiring me through grad school and beyond. Thanks to my wife, Elizabeth, for (in no particular order) her love and support and skillful editing. And thanks to Zoe for making my life matter more and my sleep matter less.

Finally I want to express my appreciation for Dr. Billi Gordon, in whose memory this book is dedicated. He was the most interesting person I'd ever met, leading a life that carried him from poverty to Hollywood to neuroscience, across gender and back again, beyond challenges most people will never have to face. We were friends and colleagues for fourteen years, but his spirit will be with me always.

References

Introduction

Lebowitz, M. S., & Ahn, W. K. (2012). Combining biomedical accounts of mental disorders with treatability information to reduce mental illness stigma. *Psychiatric Services, 63*(5), 496–499.

Lebowitz, M. S., & Ahn, W. K. (2015). Emphasizing malleability in the biology of depression: Durable effects on perceived agency and prognostic pessimism. *Behaviour Research and Therapy, 71*, 125–130.

Chapter 1

Avery, J. A., Drevets, W. C., Moseman, S. E., Bodurka, J., Barcalow, J. C., & Simmons, W. K. (2014). Major depressive disorder is associated with abnormal interoceptive activity and functional connectivity in the insula. *Biological Psychiatry, 76*(3), 258–266.

Baur, V., Hänggi, J., Langer, N., & Jäncke, L. (2013). Resting-state functional and structural connectivity within an insula-amygdala route specifically index state and trait anxiety. *Biological Psychiatry, 73*(1), 85–92.

Ichesco, E., Quintero, A., Clauw, D. J., Peltier, S., Sundgren, P. M., Gerstner, G. E., & Schmidt-Wilcke, T. (2012). Altered functional connectivity between the insula and the cingulate cortex in patients with temporomandibular disorder: A pilot study. *Headache, 52*(3), 441–454.

Lamers, F., van Oppen, P., Comijs, H. C., Smit, J. H., Spinhoven, P., van Balkom, A. J., ... Penninx, B. W. (2011). Comorbidity patterns of anxiety and depressive disorders in a large cohort study: The Netherlands Study of Depression and Anxiety (NESDA). *Journal of Clinical Psychiatry, 72*(3), 341–348.

Lebowitz, M. S., & Ahn, W. K. (2015). Emphasizing malleability in the biology of depression: Durable effects on perceived agency and prognostic pessimism. *Behaviour Research and Therapy, 71*, 125–130.

Lieberman, M.D., Eisenberger, N.I., Crockett, M. J., Tom, S. M., Pfeifer, J. H., & Way, B. M. (2007). Putting feelings into words: Affect labeling disrupts amygdala activity in response to affective stimuli. *Psychological Science, 18*(5), 421–428.

Lyubomirsky, S. (2008). *The how of happiness: A scientific approach to getting the life you want.* New York: Penguin Press.

Miller, C.W.T. (2017). Epigenetic and neural circuitry landscape of psychotherapeutic interventions. *Psychiatry Journal, 2017*, article 5491812.

Chapter 2

Dichter, G. S., Felder, J. N., Petty, C., Bizzell, J. Ernst, M., & Smoski, M. J. (2009). The effects of psychotherapy on neural responses to rewards in major depression. *Biological Psychiatry, 66*(9): 886–897.

Ochsner, K. N., Ray, R. D., Cooper, J. C., Robertson, E. R., Chopra, S., Gabrieli, J. D., & Gross, J. J. (2004). For better or for worse: Neural systems supporting the cognitive down- and up-regulation of negative emotion. *Neuroimage, 23*(2): 483–499.

Chapter 3

Boecker, H., Sprenger, T., Spilker, M. E., Henriksen, G., Koppenhoefer, M., Wagner, K. J., … Tolle, T. R. (2008). The runner's high: Opioidergic mechanisms in the human brain. *Cerebral Cortex, 18*(11), 2523–2531.

Butler, R. N. 1978. Public interest report no. 23: Exercise, the neglected therapy. *The International Journal of Aging and Human Development 8*(2): 193–195.

Buxton, O. M., Lee, C. W., L'Hermite-Baleriaux, M., Turek, F. W., & Van Cauter, E. (2003). Exercise elicits phase shifts and acute alterations of melatonin that vary with circadian phase. *American Journal of Physiology. Regulatory, Integrative and Comparative Physiology, 284*(3), R714–R724.

Frazao, D. T., de Farias Junior, L. F., Batista Dantas, T. C. B., Krinski, K., Elsangedy, H. M., Prestes, J., … Costa, E. C. (2016). Feeling of pleasure to high-intensity interval exercise is dependent of the number of work bouts and physical activity status. *PLoS One, 11*(3), e0152752.

Greenwood, B. N., Foley, T. E., Le, T. V., Strong, P. V., Loughridge, A. B., Day, H. E., & Fleshner, M. (2011). Long-term voluntary wheel running is rewarding and produces plasticity in the mesolimbic reward pathway. *Behavioural Brain Research, 217*(2), 354–362.

Hansen, C. J., Stevens, L. C., & Coast, J. R. 2001. Exercise duration and mood state: How much is enough to feel better? *Health Psychology, 20*(4): 267–275.

Helgadóttir, B., Hallgren, M., Ekblom, O., & Forsell, Y. 2016. Training fast or slow? Exercise for depression: A randomized controlled trial. *Preventive Medicine, 91*, 123–131.

Jacobs, B. L., & Fornal, C. A. (1999). Activity of serotonergic neurons in behaving animals. *Neuropsychopharmacology, 21*(2 Suppl), 9S–15S.

Janse Van Rensburg, K., Taylor, A., Hodgson, T., & Benattayallah, A. (2009). Acute exercise modulates cigarette cravings and brain activation in response to smoking-related images: An fMRI study. *Psychopharmacology, 203*(3), 589–598.

Karageorghis, C. I., Mouzourides, D. A., Priest, D. L., Sasso, T. A., Morrish, D. J., & Walley, C. J. (2009). Psychophysical and ergogenic effects of synchronous music during treadmill walking. *Journal of Sport and Exercise Psychology, 31*(1), 18–36.

Melancon, M. O., Lorrain, D., & Dionne, I. J. (2014). Changes in markers of brain serotonin activity in response to chronic exercise in senior men. *Applied Physiology, Nutrition, and Metabolism, 39*(11), 1250–1256.

Nabkasorn, C., Miyai, N., Sootmongkol, A., Junprasert, S., Yamamoto, H., Arita, M., & Miyashita, K. (2006). Effects of physical exercise on depression, neuroendocrine stress hormones and physiological fitness in adolescent females with depressive symptoms. *European Journal of Public Health, 16*(2), 179–184.

Olson, A.K., Eadie, B.D., Ernst, C., & Christie, B. R. (2006). Environmental enrichment and voluntary exercise massively increase neurogenesis in the adult hippocampus via dissociable pathways. *Hippocampus, 16*(3), 250–260.

Rethorst, C. D., & Trivedi, M. H. (2013). Evidence-based recommendations for the prescription of exercise for major depressive disorder. *Journal of Psychiatric Practice, 19*(3), 204–212.

Schachter, C. L., Busch, A. J., Peloso, P. M., & Sheppard, M. S. 2003. Effects of short versus long bouts of aerobic exercise in sedentary women with fibromyalgia: A randomized controlled trial. *Physical Therapy, 83*(4), 340–358.

Sparling, P. B., Giuffrida, A., Piomelli, D., Rosskopf, L., & Dietrich, A. (2003). Exercise activates the endocannabinoid system. *Neuroreport, 14*(17), 2209–2211.

Chapter 4

Bernardi, L., Porta, C., Casucci, G., Balsamo, R., Bernardi, N. F., Fogari, R., & Sleight, P. (2009). Dynamic interactions between musical, cardiovascular, and cerebral rhythms in humans. *Circulation, 119*(25), 3171–3180.

Blood, J. D., Wu, J., Chaplin, T. M., Hommer, R., Vazquez, L., Rutherford, H. J., … Crowley, M. J. (2015). The variable heart: High frequency and very low frequency correlates of depressive symptoms in children and adolescents. *Journal of Affective Disorders, 186*, 119–126.

Blood, A. J., & Zatorre, R. J. (2001). Intensely pleasurable responses to music correlate with activity in brain regions implicated in reward and emotion. *Proceedings of the National Academy of Sciences, 98*(20), 11818–11823.

Chen, Y.F., Huang, X.Y., Chien, C. H., & Cheng, J. F. (2017). The effectiveness of diaphragmatic breathing relaxation training for reducing anxiety. *Perspectives in psychiatric care, 53*(4), 329–336.

Coles, N., Larsen, J., & Lench, H. (2017). A meta-analysis of the facial feedback hypothesis literature. PsyArXiv preprint.

Cramer, H., Lauche, R., Langhorst, J., & Dobos, G. (2013). Yoga for depression: A systematic review and metae relaxation. *Depression and Anxiety, 30*(11), 1068–1083.

Crowther, J. H. (1983). Stress management training and relaxation imagery in the treatment of essential hypertension. *Journal of Behavioral Medicine, 6*(2), 169–187.

de Manincor, M., Bensoussan, A., Smith, C. A., Barr, K. Schweickle, M., Donoghoe, L. L., … Fahey, P. (2016). Individualized yoga for reducing depression and anxiety, and improving well-being. A randomized controlled trial. *Depression and Anxiety, 33*(9), 816–828.

Eda, N., Ito, H., Shimizu, K., Suzuki, S., Lee, E., & Akama, T. (2018). Yoga stretching for improving salivary immune function and mental stress in middle-aged and older adults. *Journal of Women and Aging, 30*(3), 227–241.

Essa, R.M., Ismail, N. I. A. A., & Hassan, N. I. (2017). Effect of progressive muscle relaxation technique on stress, anxiety, and depression after hysterectomy. *Journal of Nursing Education and Practice, 7*(7), 77.

Fung, C.N., & White, R. (2012). Systematic review of the effectiveness of relaxation training for depression. *International Journal of Applied Psychology, 2*(2), 8–16.

Jacobson, E. (1925). Progressive relaxation. *The American Journal of Psychology, 36*, 73–87.

Janssen, C.W., Lowry, C.A., Mehl, M. R., Allen, J. J., Kelly, K. L., Gartner, D. E., … Raison, C. L. (2016). Whole-body hyperthermia for the treatment of major depressive disorder: A randomized clinical trial. *JAMA Psychiatry, 73*(8), 789–795.

Kato, K., & Kanosue, K. (2018). Motor imagery of voluntary muscle relaxation of the foot induces a temporal reduction of corticospinal excitability in the hand. *Neuroscience Letters, 668*, 67–72.

Knight, W. E., & Rickard, N. S. (2001). Relaxing music prevents stress-induced increases in subjective anxiety, systolic blood pressure, and heart rate in healthy males and females. *Journal of Music Therapy, 38*(4), 254–272.

Kobayashi, S., & Koitabashi, K. (2016). Effects of progressive muscle relaxation on cerebral activity: an fMRI investigation. *Complementary Therapies in Medicine, 26*, 33–39.

Ma, X., Yue, Z.-Q., Gong, Z. Q., Zhang, H., Duan, N. Y., Shi, Y. T., … Li, Y. F. (2017). The effect of diaphragmatic breathing on attention, negative affect and stress in healthy adults. *Frontiers in Psychology, 8*, 874.

Marzoli, D., Custodero, M., Pagliara, A., & Tommasi, L. (2013). Sun-induced frowning fosters aggressive feelings. *Cognition and Emotion, 27*(8), 1513–1521.

Michalak, J., Mischnat, J., & Teismann, T. (2014). Sitting posture makes a difference-embodiment effects on depressive memory bias. *Clinical Psychology and Psychotherapy, 21*(6), 519–524.

Nakahara, H., Furuya, S., Obata, S., Masuko, T., & Kinoshita, H. (2009). Emotion-related changes in heart rate and its variability during performance and perception of music. *Annals of the New York Academy of Sciences, 1169*(1), 359–362.

Nilsson, U. (2009). Soothing music can increase oxytocin levels during bed rest after open-heart surgery: A randomised control trial. *Journal of Clinical Nursing, 18*(15), 2153–2161.

Peña, J., & Chen, M. (2017). Playing with power: Power poses affect enjoyment, presence, controller responsiveness, and arousal when playing natural motion-controlled video games. *Computers in Human Behavior, 71*, 428–435.

Russell, M. E., Scott, A. B., Boggero, I. A., & Carlson, C. R. (2017). Inclusion of a rest period in diaphragmatic breathing increases high frequency heart rate variability: Implications for behavioral therapy. *Psychophysiology, 54*(3), 358–365.

Shapiro, D., & Cline, K. (2004). Mood changes associated with Iyengar yoga practices: A pilot study. *International Journal of Yoga Therapy, 14*(1), 35–44.

Smith, K. M., & Apicella, C. L. (2017). Winners, losers, and posers: The effect of power poses on testosterone and risk-taking following competition. *Hormones and Behavior, 92*, 172–181.

Streeter, C.C., Gerbarg, P.L., Saper, R. B., Ciarulo, D. A., & Brown, R. P. (2012). Effects of yoga on the autonomic nervous system, gamma-aminobutyric-acid, and allostasis in epilepsy, depression, and post-traumatic stress disorder. *Medical Hypotheses, 78*(5), 571–579.

Thibault, R. T., Lifshitz, M., Jones, J. M., & Raz, A. (2014). Posture alters human resting-state. *Cortex, 58*, 199–205.

Törnberg, D., Marteus, H., Schedin, U., Alving, K., Lundberg, J. O., Weitzberg, E. (2002). Nasal and oral contribution to inhaled and exhaled nitric oxide: A study in tracheotomized patients. *The European Respiratory Journal, 19*(5), 859–864.

Tsai, H.-Y., Peper, E., & Lin, I.-M. (2016). EEG patterns under positive/negative body postures and emotion recall tasks. *NeuroRegulation, 3*(1), 23–27.

Villemure, C., Čeko, M., Cotton, V. A., & Bushnell, M. C. (2014). Insular cortex mediates increased pain tolerance in yoga practitioners. *Cerebral Cortex, 24*(10), 2732–2740.

Villemure, C., Čeko, M., Cotton, V. A., & Bushnell, M. C. (2015). Neuroprotective effects of yoga practice: Age-, experience-, and frequency-dependent plasticity. *Frontiers in Human Neuroscience, 9*, 281.

Wilkes, C., Kydd, R., Sagar, M., & Broadbent, E. (2017). Upright posture improves affect and fatigue in people with depressive symptoms. *Journal of Behavior Therapy and Experimental Psychiatry, 54*, 143–149.

Chapter 5

Altena, E., Van Der Werf, Y. D., Sanz-Arigita, E. J., Voorn, T. A., Rombouts, S. A., Kuijer, J. P., & Van Someren, E. J. (2008). Prefrontal hypoactivation and recovery in insomnia. *Sleep, 31*(9), 1271–1276.

Campbell, C. M., Bounds, S. C., Kuwabara, H., Edwards, R. R., Campbell, J. N., Haythornthwaite, J. A., & Smith, M. T. (2013). Individual variation in sleep quality and duration is related to cerebral mu opioid receptor binding potential during tonic laboratory pain in healthy subjects. *Pain Medicine, 14*(12), 1882–1892.

Kim, Y., Chen, L., McCarley, R. W., & Strecker, R. E. (2013). Sleep allostasis in chronic sleep restriction: The role of the norepinephrine system. *Brain Research, 1531*, 9–16.

Lopresti, A. L., Hood, S. D., & Drummond, P. D. (2013). A review of lifestyle factors that contribute to important pathways associated with major depression: Diet, sleep and exercise. *Journal of Affective Disorders, 148*(1), 12–27.

Meerlo, P., Havekes, R., & Steiger, A. (2015). Chronically restricted or disrupted sleep as a causal factor in the development of depression. *Current Topics in Behavioral Neurosciences, 25*, 459–481.

Memarian, N., Torre, J. B., Halton, K. E., Stanton, A. L., & Lieberman, M. D. (2017). Neural activity during affect labeling predicts expressive writing effects on well-being: GLM and SVM approaches. *Social Cognitive and Affective Neuroscience, 12*(9), 1437–1447.

Perlis, M. L., Jungquist, C., Smith, M. T., & Posner, D. (2006). *Cognitive behavioral treatment of insomnia: A session-by-session guide.* New York: Springer-Verlag.

Roehrs, T., Hyde, M., Blaisdell, B., Greenwald, M., & Roth, T. (2006). Sleep loss and REM sleep loss are hyperalgesic. *Sleep, 29*(2), 145–151.

Scullin, M. K., Krueger, M. L., Ballard, H. K., Pruett, N., & Bliwise, D. L. (2018). The effects of bedtime writing on difficulty falling asleep: A polysomnographic study comparing to-do lists and completed activity lists. *Journal of Experimental Psychology: General, 147*(1), 139–146.

Sivertsen, B., Salo, P., Mykeltun, A., Hysing, M., Pallesen, S., Krokstad, S., ... Øverland, S. (2012). The bidirectional association between depression and insomnia: The HUNT study. *Psychosomatic Medicine, 74*(7), 758–765.

St-Onge, M. P., Wolfe, S., Sy, M., Shechter, A., & Hirsch, J. (2014). Sleep restriction increases the neuronal response to unhealthy food in normal-weight individuals. *International Journal of Obesity, 38*(3), 411–416.

Strand, L. B., Tsai, M. K., Gunnell, D., Janszky, I., Wen, C. P., & Chang, S. S. (2016). Self-reported sleep duration and coronary heart disease mortality: A large cohort study of 400,000 Taiwanese adults. *International Journal of Cardiology, 207*, 246–251.

Wierzynski, C. M., Lubenov, E. V., Gu, M., & Siapas, A. G. (2009). State-dependent spike-timing relationships between hippocampal and prefrontal circuits during sleep. *Neuron, 61*(4), 587–596.

Xie, L., Kang, H., Xu, Q., Chen, M. J., Liao, Y., Thiyagarajan, M., ... Nedergaard, M. (2013). Sleep drives metabolite clearance from the adult brain. *Science, 342*(6156), 373–377.

Chapter 6

Aydin, N., Krueger, J. I., Fischer, J., Hahn, D., Kastenmüller, A., Frey, D., & Fischer, P. (2012). "Man's best friend": How the presence of a dog reduces mental distress after social exclusion. *Journal of Experimental Social Psychology, 48*(1), 446–449.

Cruwys, T., Dingle, G. A., Haslam, C., Haslam, S. A., Jetten, J., & Morton, T. A. (2013). Social group memberships protect against future depression, alleviate depression symptoms and prevent depression relapse. *Social Science and Medicine, 98*, 179–186.

Cruwys, T., Haslam, S. A., Dingle, G. A., Jetten, J., Hornsey, M. J., Desdemona Chong, E. M., & Oei, T. P S. (2014). Feeling connected again: Interventions that increase social identification reduce depression symptoms in community and clinical settings. *Journal of Affective Disorders, 159*, 139–146.

Dingle, G. A., Stark, C., Cruwys, T., & Best, D. (2015). Breaking good: Breaking ties with social groups may be good for recovery from substance misuse. *British Journal of Social Psychology, 54*(2), 236–254.

Eisenberger, N. I., Jarcho, J. M., Lieberman, M. D., & Naliboff, B. D. (2006). An experimental study of shared sensitivity to physical pain and social rejection. *Pain, 126*(1–3), 132–138.

Greenaway, K. H., Haslam, S. A., Cruwys, T., Branscombe, N. R., Ysseldyk, R., & Heldreth, C. (2015). From "we" to "me": Group identification enhances perceived personal control with consequences for health and well-being. *Journal of Personality and Social Psychology, 109*(1), 53–74.

Grewen, K. M., Girdler, S. S., Amico, J., & Light, K. C. (2005). Effects of partner support on resting oxytocin, cortisol, norepinephrine, and blood pressure before and after warm partner contact. *Psychosomatic Medicine, 67*(4), 531–538.

Karremans, J. C., Heslenfeld, D. J., van Dillen, L. F., & Van Lange, P. A. (2011). Secure attachment partners attenuate neural responses to social exclusion: An fMRI investigation. *International Journal of Psychophysiology, 81*(1), 44–50.

Kim, J.-W., Kim, S.-E., Kim, J. J., Jeong, B., Park, C. H., Son, A. R., ... Ki, S. W. (2009). Compassionate attitude towards others' suffering activates the mesolimbic neural system. *Neuropsychologia, 47*(10): 2073–2081.

Kumar, P., Waiter, G. D., Dubois, M., Milders, M., Reid, I., & Steele, J. D. (2017). Increased neural response to social rejection in major depression. *Depression and Anxiety, 34*(11), 1049–1056.

Masi, C. M., Chen, H.-Y., Hawkley, L. C., & Cacioppo, J. T. (2011). A meta-analysis of interventions to reduce loneliness. *Personality and Social Psychology Review, 15*(3), 219–266.

Masten, C. L., Eisenberger, N. I., Borofsky, L. A., McNealy, K., Pfeifer, J. H., & Dapretto M. (2011). Subgenual anterior cingulate responses to peer rejection: A marker of adolescents' risk for depression. *Development and Psychopathology, 23*(1), 283–292.

McQuaid, R. J., McInnis, O. A., Abizaid, A., & Anisman, H. (2014). Making room for oxytocin in understanding depression. *Neuroscience and Biobehavioral Reviews, 45*, 305–322.

Park, S. Q., Kahnt, T., Dogan, A., Strang, S., Fehr, E., & Tobler, P. N. (2017). A neural link between generosity and happiness. *Nature Communications, 8*, article 15964.

Przybylski, A. K., & Weinstein, N. (2013). Can you connect with me now? How the presence of mobile communication technology influences face-to-face conversation quality. *Journal of Social and Personal Relationships, 30*(3), 237–246.

Seymour-Smith, M., Cruwys, T., Haslam, S. A., & Brodribb, W. (2017). Loss of group memberships predicts depression in postpartum mothers. *Social Psychiatry and Psychiatric Epidemiology, 52*(2), 201–210.

Sherman, L. E., Michikyan, M., & Greenfield, P. M. (2013). The effects of text, audio, video, and in-person communication on bonding between friends. *Cyberpsychology: Journal of Psychosocial Research on Cyberspace, 7*(2), article 3.

Stone, D., Patton, B. & Heen, S. (2010). *Difficult conversations: How to discuss what matters most* (Updated ed.) New York: Penguin Books.

van Winkel, M., Wichers, M., Collip, D., Jacobs, N., Derom, C., Thiery, E. ... Peeters, F. (2017). Unraveling the role of loneliness in depression: The relationship between daily life experience and behavior. *Psychiatry, 80*(2), 104–117.

Chapter 7

Alexander, L. F., Oliver, A., Burdine, L. K., Tang, Y. & Dunlop, B. W. (2017). Reported maladaptive decision-making in unipolar and bipolar depression and its change with treatment. *Psychiatry Research, 257*: 386–392.

Barth, J., Munder, T., Gerger, H., Nüesch, E., Trelle, S., Znoj, H., ... Cuijpers, P. (2013). Comparative efficacy of seven psychotherapeutic interventions for patients with depression: A network meta-analysis. *PLoS Med, 10*(5): e1001454.

Bruine de Bruin, W., Parker, A.M., & Strough, J. (2016). Choosing to be happy? Age differences in "maximizing" decision strategies and experienced emotional well-being. *Psychology and Aging, 31*(3): 295–300.

Creswell, J. D., Welch, W. T., Taylor, S. E., Sherman, D. K., Gruenewald, T. L., & Mann, T. (2005). Affirmation of personal values buffers neuroendocrine and psychological stress responses. *Psychological Science, 16*(11): 846–851.

Etkin, J., & Mogilner, C. (2016). Does variety among activities increase happiness? *Journal of Consumer Research, 43*(2): 210–229.

Leykin, Y., Roberts, C. S., & DeRubeis, R. J. (2011). Decision-making and depressive symptomatology. *Cognitive Therapy and Research, 35*(4): 333–341.

Loveday, P. M., Lovell, G. P., & Jones, C. M. (2016). The best possible selves intervention: A review of the literature to evaluate efficacy and guide future research. *Journal of Happiness Studies, 19*(2): 607–628.

Luo, Y., Chen, X., Qi, S., You, X, & Huang, X. (2018). Well-being and anticipation for future positive events: Evidences from an fMRI study. *Frontiers in Psychology, 8*: 2199.

Rogers, R. D. (2011). The roles of dopamine and serotonin in decision making: Evidence from pharmacological experiments in humans. *Neuropsychopharmacology, 36*(1): 114–132.

Chapter 8

Fledderus, M., Bohlmeijer, E. T., Pieterse, M. E., & Schreurs, K. M. (2012). Acceptance and commitment therapy as guided self-help for psychological distress and positive mental health: A randomized controlled trial. *Psychological Medicine, 42*(3), 485–495.

Goldberg, S. B., Tucker, R. P., Greene, P. A., Davidson, R. J., Wampold, B. E., Kearney, D. J., & Simpson, T. L. (2017). Mindfulness-based interventions for psychiatric disorders: A systematic review and meta-analysis. *Clinical Psychology Review 59*, 52–60.

Gotink, R. A., Meijboom, R., Vernooij, M. W., Smits, M., & Hunink, M. G. (2016). 8-week mindfulness based stress reduction induces brain changes similar to traditional long-term meditation practice: A systematic review. *Brain and Cognition, 108*, 32–41.

Joiner, T. (2017). *Mindlessness: The corruption of mindfulness in a culture of narcissism.* Oxford, UK: Oxford University Press.

Kirk, U., & Montague, P. R. (2015). Mindfulness meditation modulates reward prediction errors in a passive conditioning task. *Frontiers in Psychology, 6*, 90.

Kuyken, W., Warren, F. C., Taylor, R. S., Whalley, B., Crane, C., Bondolfi, G., … Dalgleish, T. (2016). Efficacy of mindfulness-based cognitive therapy in prevention of depressive relapse: An individual patient data meta-analysis from randomized trials. *JAMA Psychiatry, 73*(6), 565–574.

Lieberman, M. D., Eisenberger, N. I., Crockett, M. J., Tom, S. M., Pfeifer, J. H., & Way, B. M. (2007). Putting feelings into words: Affect labeling disrupts amygdala activity in response to affective stimuli. *Psychological Science, 18*(5): 421–428.

Lindsay, E. K., Young, S., Smyth, J. M., Brown, K. W., & Creswell, J. D. (2018). Acceptance lowers stress reactivity: Dismantling mindfulness training in a randomized controlled trial. *Psychoneuroendocrinology, 87*, 63–73.

Mrazek, M. D., Franklin, M. S., Phillips, D. T., Baird, B., & Schooler, J. W. (2013). Mindfulness training improves working memory capacity and GRE performance while reducing mind wandering. *Psychological Science, 24*(5), 776–781.

Posner, M. I., Tang, Y.-Y., & Lynch, G. (2014). Mechanisms of white matter change induced by meditation training. *Frontiers in Psychology, 5,* 1220.

Salomons, T. V., Johnstone, T., Backonja, M. M., Shackman, A. J., & Davidson, R. J. (2007). Individual differences in the effects of perceived controllability on pain perception: Critical role of the prefrontal cortex. *Journal of Cognitive Neuroscience, 19*(6), 993–1003.

Strauss, C., Cavanagh, K., Oliver, A., & Pettman, D. (2014). Mindfulness-based interventions for people diagnosed with a current episode of an anxiety or depressive disorder: A meta-analysis of randomised controlled trials. *PLoS One, 9*(4), e96110.

Tang, Y.-Y., Hölzel, B. K., & Posner, M. I. (2015). The neuroscience of mindfulness meditation. *Nature Reviews Neuroscience, 16*(4), 213–225.

Visted, E., Sørensen, L., Osnes, B., Svendsen, J. L., Binder, P. E., & Schanche, E. (2017). The association between self-reported difficulties in emotion regulation and heart rate variability: The salient role of not accepting negative emotions. *Frontiers in Psychology, 8,* 328.

Wiech, K., Kalisch, R., Weiskopf, N., Pleger, B., Stephan, K. E., & Dolan, R. J. (2006). Anterolateral prefrontal cortex mediates the analgesic effect of expected and perceived control over pain. *The Journal of Neuroscience, 26*(44), 11501–11509.

Wilson, T. D., Reinhard, D. A., Westgate, E. C., Gilbert, D. T., Ellerbeck, N., Hahn, C., ... & Shaked, A. (2014). Just think: The challenges of the disengaged mind. *Science, 345*(6192), 75–77.

Winnebeck, E., Fissler, M., Gärtner, M., Chadwick, P., & Barnhofer, T. (2017). Brief training in mindfulness meditation reduces symptoms in patients with a chronic or recurrent lifetime history of depression: A randomized controlled study. *Behavior Research and Therapy, 99,* 124–130.

Young, K. S., van der Velden, A. M., Craske, M. G., Pallesen, K. J., Fjorback, L., Roepstorff, A., & Parsons, C. E. (2018). The impact of mindfulness-based interventions on brain activity: A systematic review of functional magnetic resonance imaging studies. *Neuroscience and Biobehavioral Reviews, 84,* 424–433.

Zeidan, F., Johnson, S. K., Gordon, N. S., & Goolkasian, P. (2010). Effects of brief and sham mindfulness meditation on mood and cardiovascular variables. *Journal of Alternative and Complementary Medicine, 16*(8), 867–873.

Zeidan, F., Martucci, K. T., Kraft, R. A., McHaffie, J. G., & Coghill, R. C. (2014). Neural correlates of mindfulness meditation-related anxiety relief. *Social Cognitive and Affective Neuroscience, 9*(6), 751–759.

Chapter 9

Carnegie, D. (2010). *How to win friends and influence people*. New York: Pocket Books.

Dutcher, J. M., Creswell, J. D., Pacilio, L. E., Harris, P. R., Klein, W. M., Levine, J. M., ... Eisenberger, N. I. (2016). Self-affirmation activates the ventral striatum: A possible reward-related mechanism for self-affirmation. *Psychological Science, 27*(4): 455–466.

Epton, T., Harris, P. R., Kane, R., van Koningsbruggen, G. M., & Sheeran, P. (2015). The impact of self-affirmation on health-behavior change: A meta-analysis. *Health Psychology, 34*(3): 187–196.

Felitti, V. J., Jakstis, K., Pepper, V., & Ray, A. (2010). Obesity: problem, solution, or both? *The Permanente Journal, 14*(1): 24–30.

Foster, J.A., & McVey Neufeld, K.-A. (2013). Gut–brain axis: How the microbiome influences anxiety and depression. *Trends in Neurosciences, 36*(5): 305–312.

Gallwey, T. W. (1997) *The inner game of tennis* (Rev. ed.). New York: Random House.

Jacka, F. N., Kremer, P. J., Berk, M., de Silva-Sanigorski, A. M., Moodie, M., Leslie, E. R., … Swinburn, B. A. (2011). A prospective study of diet quality and mental health in adolescents. *PLoS One, 6*(9), e24805.

Jacka, F. N., O'Neil, A., Opie, R., Itsiopoulos, C., Cotton, S., Mohebbi, M., … Berk, M. (2017). A randomised controlled trial of dietary improvement for adults with major depression (the "SMILES" trial). *BMC Medicine, 15*(1): 23.

Kuroda, A., Tanaka, T., Hirano, H., Ohara, Y., Kikutani, T., Furuya, H., … Iijima, K. (2015). Eating alone as social disengagement is strongly associated with depressive symptoms in Japanese community-dwelling older adults. *Journal of the American Medical Directors Association, 16*(7): 578–585.

Longe, O., Maratos, F. A., Gilbert, P., Evans, G., Volker, F., Rockliff, H., & Rippon, G. (2010). Having a word with yourself: Neural correlates of self-criticism and self-reassurance. *Neuroimage, 49*(2), 1849–1856.

Rada, P., Avena, N., & Hoebel, B. (2005). Daily bingeing on sugar repeatedly releases dopamine in the accumbens shell. *Neuroscience, 134*(3): 737–744.

Winkens, L., van Strien, T., Brouwer, I. A., Penninx, B. W. J. H., Visser, M., & Lähteenmäki, L. (2018). Associations of mindful eating domains with depressive symptoms and depression in three European countries. *Journal of Affective Disorders, 228*: 26–32.

Chapter 10

Bartolo, A., Benuzzi, F., Nocetti, L., Baraldi, P., & Nichelli, P. (2006). Humor comprehension and appreciation: An FMRI study. *Journal of Cognitive Neuroscience, 18*(11): 1789–1798.

Berman, M. G., Kross, E., Krpan, K. M., Askren, M. K., Burson, A., Deldin, P. J., … Jonides, J. (2012). Interacting with nature improves cognition and affect for individuals with depression. *Journal of Affective Disorders, 140*(3): 300–305.

Billingsley, J., & Losin, E. A. (2017). The neural systems of forgiveness: an evolutionary psychological perspective. *Frontiers in Psychology, 8*: 737.

Chaves, C., Lopez-Gomez, I., Hervas, G., & Vazquez, C. (2017). A comparative study on the efficacy of a positive psychology intervention and a cognitive behavioral therapy for clinical depression. *Cognitive Therapy and Research, 41*(3): 417–433.

Chirico, A., Cipresso, P., Yaden, D. B., Biassoni, F., Riva, G., & Gaggioli, A. (2017). Effectiveness of immersive videos in inducing awe: An experimental study. *Scientific Reports, 7*(1): 1218.

Disabato, D. J., Kashdan, T. B., Short, J. L., & Jarden, A. (2017). What predicts positive life events that influence the course of depression? A longitudinal examination of gratitude and meaning in life. *Cognitive Therapy and Research, 41*(3): 444–458.

Fatfouta, R., Meshi, D., Merkl, A., & Heekeren, H. R. (2018). Accepting unfairness by a significant other is associated with reduced connectivity between medial prefrontal and dorsal anterior cingulate cortex. *Social Neuroscience, 13*(1): 61–73.

Fox, G. R., Kaplan, J., Damasio, H., & Damasio, A. (2015). Neural correlates of gratitude. *Frontiers in Psychology, 6*: 1491.

Gonçalves, J. P., Lucchetti, G., Menezes, P. R., & Vallada, H. (2015). Religious and spiritual interventions in mental health care: A systematic review and meta-analysis of randomized controlled clinical trials. *Psychological Medicine, 45*(14): 2937–2949.

Hill, P. L., Allemand, M., & Roberts, B. W. (2013). Examining the pathways between gratitude and self-rated physical health across adulthood. *Personality and Individual Differences, 54*(1), 92–96.

Ishizu, T., & Zeki, S. (2014). A neurobiological enquiry into the origins of our experience of the sublime and beautiful. *Frontiers in Human Neuroscience, 8*: 891.

Joye, Y., & Bolderdijk, J. W. (2015). An exploratory study into the effects of extraordinary nature on emotions, mood, and prosociality. *Frontiers in Psychology, 5*: 1577.

Karns, C. M., Moore, W. E., III, & Mayr, U. (2017). The cultivation of pure altruism via gratitude: A functional MRI study of change with gratitude practice. *Frontiers in Human Neuroscience, 11*: 599.

Kerr, S. L., O'Donovan, A., & Pepping, C. A. (2015). Can gratitude and kindness interventions enhance well-being in a clinical sample? *Journal of Happiness Studies, 16*(1): 17–36.

Kini, P., Wong, J., McInnis, S., Gabana, N., & Brown, J. W. (2016). The effects of gratitude expression on neural activity. *Neuroimage, 128*: 1–10.

Koh, A. H., Tong, E. M. W., & Yuen, A. Y. L. (2017). The buffering effect of awe on negative affect towards lost possessions. *The Journal of Positive Psychology, 9760*: 1–10.

Lin, C.-C. (2015). Gratitude and depression in young adults: The mediating role of self-esteem and well-being. *Personality and Individual Differences, 87*: 30–34.

Lyubomirsky, S., Sousa, L., & Dickerhoof, R. (2006). The costs and benefits of writing, talking, and thinking about life's triumphs and defeats. *Journal of Personality and Social Psychology, 90*(4): 692–708.

McCullough, M. E., Root, L. M., & Cohen, A. D. (2006). Writing about the benefits of an interpersonal transgression facilitates forgiveness. *Journal of Consulting and Clinical Psychology, 74*(5): 887–897.

McMahan, E. A., & Estes, D. (2015). The effect of contact with natural environments on positive and negative affect: A meta-analysis. *The Journal of Positive Psychology, 10*(6): 507–519.

Mobbs, D., Greicius, M. D., Abdel-Azim, E., Menon, V., & Reiss, A. L. (2003). Humor modulates the mesolimbic reward centers. *Neuron, 40*(5): 1041–1048.

Muris, P., & Petrocchi, N. (2017). Protection or vulnerability? A meta-analysis of the relations between the positive and negative components of self-compassion and psychopathology. *Clinical Psychology and Psychotherapy, 24*(2): 373–383.

Passmore, H.-A., & Howell, A. J. 2014. Nature involvement increases hedonic and eudaimonic well-being: A two-week experimental study. *Ecopsychology, 6*(3): 148–154.

Perreau-Linck, E., Beauregard, M., Gravel, P., Paquette, V., Soucy. J. P., Diksic. M., & Benkelfat, C. (2007). In vivo measurements of brain trapping of C-labelled alpha-methyl-L-tryptophan during acute changes in mood states. *Journal of Psychiatry and Neuroscience, 32*(6): 430–434.

Petrocchi, N., & Couyoumdjian, A. (2016). The impact of gratitude on depression and anxiety: The mediating role of criticizing, attacking, and reassuring the self. *Self and Identity, 15*(2): 191–205.

Redwine, L. S., Henry, B. L., Pung, M. A., Wilson, K., Chinh, K., Knight, B. … Mills, P. J. (2016). Pilot randomized study of a gratitude journaling intervention on heart rate variability and inflammatory biomarkers in patients with stage B heart failure. *Psychosomatic Medicine, 78*(6): 667–676.

Reed, G. L., & Enright, R. D. (2006). The effects of forgiveness therapy on depression, anxiety, and post-traumatic stress for women after spousal emotional abuse. *Journal of Consulting and Clinical Psychology, 74*(5): 920–929.

Rudd, M., Vohs, K. D., & Aaker, J. (2012). Awe expands people's perception of time, alters decision making, and enhances well-being. *Psychological Science, 23*(10): 1130–1136.

Shiota, M. N., Neufeld, S .L., Yeung, W. H., Moser, S. E., & Perea, E. F. (2011). Feeling good: Autonomic nervous system responding in five positive emotions. *Emotion, 11*(6): 1368–1378.

Siep, N., Roefs, A., Roebroeck, A., Havermans, R., Bonte, M. L., & Jansen, A. (2009). Hunger is the best spice: An fMRI study of the effects of attention, hunger and calorie content on food reward processing in the amygdala and orbitofrontal cortex. *Behavioural Brain Research, 198*(1): 149–158.

Sin, N. L., & Lyubomirsky, S. (2009). Enhancing well-being and alleviating depressive symptoms with positive psychology interventions: A practice-friendly meta-analysis. *Journal of Clinical Psychology, 65*(5): 467–487.

Speer, M. E., Bhanji, J. P., & Delgado, M. R. (2014). Savoring the past: Positive memories evoke value representations in the striatum. *Neuron, 84*(4): 847–856.

Stellar, J. E., Gordon, A. M., Piff, P. K., Cordaro, D., Anderson, C. L., Bai, Y., … Keltner, D. (2017). Self-transcendent emotions and their social functions: Compassion, gratitude, and awe bind us to others through prosociality. *Emotion Review, 9*(3): 200–207.

vanOyen Witvliet, C., Root Luna, L., VanderStoep, J. V., Vlisides-Henry, R. D., Gonzalez, T., & Griffin, G. D. (2018). OXTR rs53576 genotype and gender predict trait gratitude. *The Journal of Positive Psychology*: 1–10.

Wellenzohn, S., Proyer, R. T., & Ruch, W. (2016). Humor-based online positive psychology interventions: A randomized placebo-controlled long-term trial. *The Journal of Positive Psychology, 11*(6): 584–594.

Wong, Y. J., Owen, J., Gabana, N. T., Brown, J. W., McInnis, S., Toth, P. & Gilman, L. (2018). Does gratitude writing improve the mental health of psychotherapy clients? Evidence from a randomized controlled trial. *Psychotherapy Research, 28*(2): 192–202.

Wood, A. M., Joseph, S., Lloyd, J., & Atkins, S. (2009). Gratitude influences sleep through the mechanism of pre-sleep cognitions. *Journal of Psychosomatic Research, 66*(1), 43–48.

Wood, A. M., Maltby, J., Gillett, R., Linley, P. A., & Joseph, S. (2008). The role of gratitude in the development of social support, stress, and depression: Two longitudinal studies. *Journal of Research in Personality, 42*(4): 854–871.

Zahn, R., Moll, J., Paivia, M., Garrido, G., Krueger, F., Huey, E. D., & Grafman, J. (2009). The neural basis of human social values: Evidence from functional MRI. *Cerebral Cortex, 19*(2): 276–283.

Chapter 11

Clever, S. L., Ford, D. E., Rubenstein, L. V., Rost, K. M., Meredith, L. S., Sherbourne, C. D., … Cooper, L. A. (2006). Primary care patients' involvement in decision-making is associated with improvement in depression. *Medical Care, 44*(5), 398–405.

Alex Korb, PhD, is a neuroscientist who has studied the brain and mental health for over fifteen years, starting with an undergraduate degree in neuroscience from Brown University. He received his PhD in neuroscience from the University of California, Los Angeles (UCLA), where he wrote his dissertation and numerous scientific articles on depression. He is author of *The Upward Spiral*, and is currently adjunct assistant professor at UCLA in the department of psychiatry. Outside of the lab, he is a scientific consultant for the biotech industry, and is head coach of the UCLA Women's Ultimate Frisbee team. He has a wealth of experience in yoga and mindfulness, physical fitness, and even stand-up comedy.

Foreword writer **Peter C. Whybrow, MD**, is director of the Semel Institute for Neuroscience and Human Behavior at the University of California, Los Angeles. Born and educated in England, he is author of, among other books, *A Mood Apart*, the award-winning *American Mania*, and *The Well-Tuned Brain*.

MORE BOOKS *from*
NEW HARBINGER PUBLICATIONS

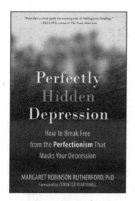

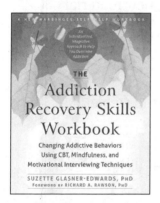

Register your **new harbinger** titles for additional benefits!

When you register your **new harbinger** title—purchased in any format, from any source—you get access to benefits like the following:

- Downloadable accessories like printable worksheets and extra content

- Instructional videos and audio files

- Information about updates, corrections, and new editions

Not every title has accessories, but we're adding new material all the time.

Access free accessories in 3 easy steps:

1. Sign in at NewHarbinger.com (or **register** to create an account).

2. Click on **register a book**. Search for your title and click the **register** button when it appears.

3. Click on the **book cover or title** to go to its details page. Click on **accessories** to view and access files.

That's all there is to it!

If you need help, visit:

NewHarbinger.com/accessories

new harbinger
CELEBRATING
40 YEARS